MznLnx

Missing Links Exam Preps

Exam Prep for

Financial and Managerial Accounting

Warren & Reeve, 9th Edition

The MznLnx Exam Prep is your link from the texbook and lecture to your exams.
The MznLnx Exam Preps are unauthorized and comprehensive reviews of your textbooks.

All material provided by MznLnx and Rico Publications (c) 2010
Textbook publishers and textbook authors do not particpate in or contribute to these reviews.

MznLnx

Rico
Publications

Exam Prep for Financial and Managerial Accounting
9th Edition
Warren & Reeve

Publisher: Raymond Houge
Assistant Editor: Michael Rouger
Text and Cover Designer: Lisa Buckner
Marketing Manager: Sara Swagger
Project Manager, Editorial Production: Jerry Emerson
Art Director: Vernon Lowerui

Product Manager: Dave Mason
Editorial Assitant: Rachel Guzmanji
Pedagogy: Debra Long
Cover Image: Jim Reed/Getty Images
Text and Cover Printer: City Printing, Inc.
Compositor: Media Mix, Inc.

(c) 2010 Rico Publications
ALL RIGHTS RESERVED. No part of this work covered by the copyright may be reproduced or used in any form or by an means--graphic, electronic, or mechanical, including photocopying, recording, taping, Web distribution, information storage, and retrieval systems, or in any other manner--without the written permission of the publisher.

Printed in the United States
ISBN:

For more information about our products, contact us at:
Dave.Mason@RicoPublications.com

For permission to use material from this text or product, submit a request online to:
Dave.Mason@RicoPublications.com

Contents

CHAPTER 1
Introduction to Accounting and Business — 1

CHAPTER 2
Analyzing Transactions — 14

CHAPTER 3
The Adjusting Process — 20

CHAPTER 4
Completing the Accounting Cycle — 25

CHAPTER 5
Accounting for Merchandising Businesses — 32

CHAPTER 6
Inventories — 40

CHAPTER 7
Sarbanes-Oxley, Internal Control, and Cash — 46

CHAPTER 8
Receivables — 52

CHAPTER 9
Fixed Assets and Intangible Assets — 57

CHAPTER 10
Current Liabilities and Payroll — 66

CHAPTER 11
Corporations: Organization, Stock Transactions, and Dividends — 76

CHAPTER 12
Income Taxes, Unusual Income Items, and Investments in Stocks — 86

CHAPTER 13
Bonds Payable and Investments in Bonds — 94

CHAPTER 14
Statement of Cash Flows — 101

CHAPTER 15
Financial Statement Analysis — 107

CHAPTER 16
Managerial Accounting Concepts and Principles — 115

CHAPTER 17
Job Order Cost Systems — 121

CHAPTER 18
Process Cost Systems — 125

CHAPTER 19
Cost Behavior and Cost-Volume-Profit Analysis — 127

CHAPTER 20
Variable Costing for Management Analysis — 131

Contents (Cont.)

CHAPTER 21
Budgeting — 135

CHAPTER 22
Performance Evaluation Using Variances from Standard Costs — 139

CHAPTER 23
Performance Evaluation for Decentralized Operations — 142

CHAPTER 24
Differential Analysis and Product Pricing — 146

CHAPTER 25
Capital Investment Analysis — 150

CHAPTER 26
Cost Allocation and Activity-Based Costing — 156

CHAPTER 27
Cost Management for Just-in-Time Environments — 159

ANSWER KEY — 164

TO THE STUDENT

COMPREHENSIVE

The *MznLnx* Exam Prep series is designed to help you pass your exams. Editors at MznLnx review your textbooks and then prepare these practice exams to help you master the textbook material. Unlike study guides, workbooks, and practice tests provided by the texbook publisher and textbook authors, *MznLnx* gives you **all** of the material in each chapter in exam form, not just samples, so you can be sure to nail your exam.

MECHANICAL

The MznLnx Exam Prep series creates exams that will help you learn the subject matter as well as test you on your understanding. Each question is designed to help you master the concept. Just working through the exams, you gain an understanding of the subject--its a simple mechanical process that produces success.

INTEGRATED STUDY GUIDE AND REVIEW

MznLnx is not just a set of exams designed to test you, its also a comprehensive review of the subject content. Each exam question is also a review of the concept, making sure that you will get the answer correct without having to go to other sources of material. You learn as you go! Its the easiest way to pass an exam.

HUMOR

Studying can be tedious and dry. MznLnx's instructional design includes moderate humor within the exam questions on occassion, to break the tedium and revitalize the brain

Chapter 1. Introduction to Accounting and Business

1. _____ in economics and business is the result of an exchange and from that trade we assign a numerical monetary value to a good, service or asset. If Alice trades Bob 4 apples for an orange, the _____ of an orange is 4 apples. Inversely, the _____ of an apple is 1/4 oranges.
   a. Resale price maintenance
   b. Pricing
   c. Transactional Net Margin Method
   d. Price

2. _____ refers to the methods, practices and operations conducted to promote and sustain certain categories of commercial activity. The term is understood to have different specific meanings depending on the context. Merchandise is a sale goods at a store

   In marketing, one of the definitions of _____ is the practice in which the brand or image from one product or service is used to sell another.

   a. 3M Company
   b. BMC Software, Inc.
   c. Merchandise
   d. Merchandising

3. A _____ is a type of business entity in which partners (owners) share with each other the profits or losses of the business undertaking in which all have invested. _____s are often favored over corporations for taxation purposes, as the _____ structure does not generally incur a tax on profits before it is distributed to the partners (i.e. there is no dividend tax levied.) However, depending on the _____ structure and the jurisdiction in which it operates, owners of a _____ may be exposed to greater personal liability than they would as shareholders of a corporation.
   a. Bond indenture
   b. Trust indenture
   c. Partnership
   d. FCPA

4. A sole _____, or simply _____ is a type of business entity which legally has no separate existence from its owner. Hence, the limitations of liability enjoyed by a corporation and limited liability partnerships do not apply to sole proprietors. All debts of the business are debts of the owner.
   a. Kaizen
   b. Product life cycle
   c. Proprietorship
   d. Pre-determined overhead rate

5. An _____ is a practitioner of accountancy, which is the measurement, disclosure or provision of assurance about financial information that helps managers, investors, tax authorities and other decision makers make resource allocation decisions.

   The word '_____' is derived from the French 'Compter' which took its origin from the Latin 'Computare'. The word was formerly written in English as 'Accomptant', but in process of time the word, which was always pronounced by dropping the 'p', became gradually changed both in pronunciation and in orthography to its present form.

   a. ABC Television Network
   b. AIG
   c. AMEX
   d. Accountant

6. _____ is a costing model that identifies activities in an organization and assigns the cost of each activity resource to all products and services according to the actual consumption by each: it assigns more indirect costs (overhead) into direct costs.

Chapter 1. Introduction to Accounting and Business

In this way an organization can establish the true cost of its individual products and services for the purposes of identifying and eliminating those which are unprofitable and lowering the prices of those which are overpriced.

In a business organization, the ABC methodology assigns an organization's resource costs through activities to the products and services provided to its customers.

- a. Activity-based management
- b. Indirect costs
- c. ABC Television Network
- d. Activity-based costing

7. In financial accounting, a _____ or statement of financial position is a summary of a person's or organization's balances. Assets, liabilities and ownership equity are listed as of a specific date, such as the end of its financial year. A _____ is often described as a snapshot of a company's financial condition.
   - a. Balance sheet
   - b. Notes to the financial statements
   - c. Statement of retained earnings
   - d. 3M Company

8. _____ is a list of the accounts including a unique number of each allowing to locate it in each ledger. The list is typically arranged in the order of the customary appearance of accounts in the financial statements. A _____ can track a specific financial information.
   - a. Chart of accounts
   - b. Journal entry
   - c. General journal
   - d. General ledger

9. _____ is concerned with the provisions and use of accounting information to managers within organizations, to provide them with the basis to make informed business decisions that will allow them to be better equipped in their management and control functions.

In contrast to financial accountancy information, _____ information is:

- usually confidential and used by management, instead of publicly reported;
- forward-looking, instead of historical;
- pragmatically computed using extensive management information systems and internal controls, instead of complying with accounting standards.

This is because of the different emphasis: _____ information is used within an organization, typically for decision-making.

- a. Nonassurance services
- b. Governmental accounting
- c. Grenzplankostenrechnung
- d. Management accounting

10. There are many _____ entity defined in the legal systems of various countries. These include corporations, partnerships, sole traders and other specialized types of organization. Some of these types are listed below, by country.
    - a. Patent
    - b. Burden of proof
    - c. Leasing
    - d. Types of Business

Chapter 1. Introduction to Accounting and Business 3

11. In economics, _____ or _____ goods or real _____ refers to factors of production used to create goods or services that are not themselves significantly consumed (though they may depreciate) in the production process. _____ goods may be acquired with money or financial _____. In finance and accounting, _____ generally refers to financial wealth, especially that used to start or maintain a business.
   a. Consumption
   b. Sale
   c. Debt-to-GDP ratios
   d. Capital

12. An _____ is a term used in behavioral economics to describe those types of behaviors that impose costs on a person in the long-run that are not taken into account when making decisions in the present. Classical Economics discourages government from creating legislation that targets internalities, because it is assumed that the consumer takes these personal costs into account when paying for the good that causes the _____. For example, cigarettes should be taxed because of the negative consumption externalities that they impose, such as second-hand smoke, not because the smoker harms him or herself by smoking.
   a. Authorised capital
   b. Inventory turnover ratio
   c. Operating budget
   d. Internality

13. _____ is a concept whereby a person's financial liability is limited to a fixed sum, most commonly the value of a person's investment in a company or partnership with _____. A shareholder in a limited company is not personally liable for any of the debts of the company, other than for the value of his investment in that company. The same is true for the members of a _____ partnership and the limited partners in a limited partnership.
   a. Burden of proof
   b. Sumptuary
   c. Staple right
   d. Limited liability

14. A _____ in the law of the vast majority of United States jurisdictions is a legal form of business company that provides limited liability to its owners. Often incorrectly called a 'limited liability corporation' (instead of company), it is a hybrid business entity having certain characteristics of both a corporation and a partnership. The primary characteristic an _____ shares with a corporation is limited liability, and the primary characteristic it shares with a partnership is the availability of pass-through income taxation.
   a. Consumer protection laws
   b. Data protection
   c. Bond market
   d. Limited liability company

15. _____ is a form of applied ethics that examines ethical principles and moral or ethical problems that arise in a business environment. It applies to all aspects of business conduct and is relevant to the conduct of individuals and business organizations as a whole. Applied ethics is a field of ethics that deals with ethical questions in many fields such as medical, technical, legal and _____.
   a. BMC Software, Inc.
   b. BNSF Railway
   c. 3M Company
   d. Business Ethics

16. _____ is the total cost involved in operating all production facilities of a manufacturing business. It generally applies to indirect labor and indirect cost, it also includes all costs involved in manufacturing with the exception of the cost of raw materials and direct labor. _____ also includes certain costs such as quality assurance costs, cleanup costs, and property insurance premiums.
   a. Cost driver
   b. Factory overhead
   c. Contribution margin analysis
   d. Profit center

Chapter 1. Introduction to Accounting and Business

17. In financial accounting, a _____ is defined as an obligation of an entity arising from past transactions or events, the settlement of which may result in the transfer or use of assets, provision of services or other yielding of economic benefits in the future.
    a. Trust Indenture Act of 1939
    b. Pre-emption right
    c. Resource Conservation and Recovery Act
    d. Liability

18. A _____ is any one of a variety of different systems, institutions, procedures, social relations and infrastructures whereby persons trade, and goods and services are exchanged, forming part of the economy. It is an arrangement that allows buyers and sellers to exchange things. _____s vary in size, range, geographic scale, location, types and variety of human communities, as well as the types of goods and services traded.
    a. Nominal value
    b. Market Failure
    c. Recession
    d. Market

19. In business, _____, Overhead cost or _____ expense refers to an ongoing expense of operating a business. The term _____ is usually used to group expenses that are necessary to the continued functioning of the business, but do not directly generate profits.

    _____ expenses are all costs on the income statement except for direct labor and direct materials.

    a. Intangible assets
    b. Overhead
    c. AIG
    d. ABC Television Network

20. The term _____ usually refers to a company that is permitted to offer its registered securities (stock, bonds, etc.) for sale to the general public, typically through a stock exchange, or occasionally a company whose stock is traded over the counter (OTC) via market makers who use non-exchange quotation services.

    The term '_____' may also refer to a company owned by the government.

    a. Public Company
    b. National Conference of Commissioners on Uniform State Laws
    c. MicroStrategy
    d. Privately held

21. The _____ (sometimes called 'Peekaboo') is a private-sector, non-profit corporation created by the Sarbanes-Oxley Act, a 2002 United States federal law, to oversee the auditors of public companies. Its stated purpose is to 'protect the interests of investors and further the public interest in the preparation of informative, fair, and independent audit reports'. Although a private entity, the _____ has many government-like regulatory functions, making it in some ways similar to the private Self Regulatory Organizations (SROs) that regulate stock markets and other aspects of the financial markets in the United States.
    a. 3M Company
    b. Financial Crimes Enforcement Network
    c. Pension Benefit Guaranty Corporation
    d. Public Company Accounting Oversight Board

22. The _____ of 2002 (Pub.L. 107-204, 116 Stat. 745, enacted July 30, 2002), also known as the Public Company Accounting Reform and Investor Protection Act of 2002, is a United States federal law enacted on July 30, 2002 in response to a number of major corporate and accounting scandals including those affecting Enron, Tyco International, Adelphia, Peregrine Systems and WorldCom. The legislation establishes new or enhanced standards for all U.S. public company boards, management, and public accounting firms. It does not apply to privately held companies.

Chapter 1. Introduction to Accounting and Business

a. Burden of proof
b. Tax lien
c. Staple right
d. Sarbanes-Oxley Act

23. _____ is the practical application of management techniques to control and report on the financial health of the organization. This involves the analysis, planning, implementation, and control of programs designed to provide financial data reporting for managerial decision making. This includes the maintenance of bank accounts, developing financial statements, cash flow and financial performance analysis.

a. Activity-based management
b. ABC Television Network
c. Activity-based costing
d. Accounting management

24. The _____ is a professional association for individuals who process company payrolls. The Association conducts payroll training courses and seminars yearly and publishes a library of payroll resource texts and newsletters. The _____ has almost 24,000 members, 149 _____-affiliated local chapters and registered lobbyists based in Washington, D.C.

a. International Federation of Accountants
b. International Accounting Standards Committee
c. Information Systems Audit and Control Association
d. American Payroll Association

25. The general definition of an _____ is an evaluation of a person, organization, system, process, project or product. _____s are performed to ascertain the validity and reliability of information; also to provide an assessment of a system's internal control. The goal of an _____ is to express an opinion on the person/organization/system (etc) in question, under evaluation based on work done on a test basis.

a. Audit
b. Institute of Chartered Accountants of India
c. Assurance service
d. Audit regime

26. _____ is a professional certification for IT audit professionals sponsored by the Information Systems Audit and Control Association (ISACA.) Candidates for the certification must meet requirements set by ISACA.

The _____ certification was established in 1978 for several reasons:

1. Develop and maintain a tool that could be used to evaluate an individuals' competency in conducting information system audits.
2. Provide a motivational tool for information systems auditors to maintain their skills, and monitor the success of the maintenance programs.
3. Provide criteria to help aid management in the selection of personnel and development.

The first _____ examination was administered in 1981, and registration numbers have grown each year. Over 60,000 candidates have earned the _____ designation.

a. Certified Information Systems Auditor
b. BMC Software, Inc.
c. 3M Company
d. BNSF Railway

27. The _____ designation is an exam-based payroll certification attained by individuals who possess a high level of professional competency through both the acquisition of knowledge and direct payroll experience.

Chapter 1. Introduction to Accounting and Business

Prior to sitting for the exam, a _____ candidate must verify employment in the payroll profession preceding the exam date. The _____ designation indicates that an individual has the experience and skills necessary to provide strategic payroll management and support to facilitate a companye;s overall business goals.

a. BNSF Railway
b. BMC Software, Inc.
c. 3M Company
d. Certified Payroll Professional

28. An _____ is an examination of the controls within an Information technology (IT) infrastructure. An IT audit is the process of collecting and evaluating evidence of an organization's information systems, practices, and operations. The evaluation of obtained evidence determines if the information systems are safeguarding assets, maintaining data integrity, and operating effectively and efficiently to achieve the organization's goals or objectives.

a. ABC Television Network
b. Information technology audit process
c. Information technology audit
d. AIG

29. ISACA is an international professional association that deals with IT Governance. It is an affiliate member of IFAC. Previously known as the _____, ISACA now goes by its acronym only, to reflect the broad range of IT governance professionals it serves.

a. American Accounting Association
b. Amoco
c. Information Systems Audit and Control Association
d. East Asia Economic Caucus

30. Established in 1941, The _____ is internationally recognized as a trustworthy guidance-setting body. Serving members in 165 countries, The IIA is the internal audit profession's global voice, chief advocate, recognized authority, acknowledged leader, and principal educator, with global headquarters in Altamonte Springs, Fla., United States.

The stated mission of The _____ is to provide dynamic leadership for the global profession of internal auditing.

a. Audit regime
b. Event data
c. Institute of Internal Auditors
d. Auditor independence

31. The _____ is a professional organization headquartered in Montvale, New Jersey consisting of over 70,000 members worldwide. The IMA is dedicated to advancing the role of the management accountant and financial manager within the business organization, and provides relevant professional certification.

The IMA awards the Certified Management Accountant (CMA) designation in the United States.

a. International Accounting Standards Committee
b. Emerging technologies
c. Institute of Management Accountants
d. American Accounting Association

32. Internal auditing is a profession and activity involved in helping organisations achieve their stated objectives. It does this by utilizing a systematic methodology for analyzing business processes, procedures and activities with the goal of highlighting organizational problems and recommending solutions. Professionals called _____ are employed by organizations to perform the internal auditing activity.

a. Auditor independence
b. Internal Auditing
c. Auditing Standards Board
d. Internal auditors

33. In a company, _____ is the sum of all financial records of salaries, wages, bonuses and deductions.

A paycheck, is traditionally a paper document issued by an employer to pay an employee for services rendered. While most commonly used in the United States, recently the physical paycheck has been increasingly replaced by electronic direct deposit to bank accounts.

a. 3M Company
b. Total Expense Ratio
c. Payroll
d. Tax expense

34. _____ is an expansion of accounting rules that goes beyond the realm of financial measures for both individual economic entities and national economies. It is advocated by those who consider the focus of the present standards and practices wholly inadequate to the task of measuring and reporting the activity, success, and failure of modern enterprise, including government.

Real debate concerns concepts such as whether to report transactions, such as asset acquisitions, at their cost or at their current market values.

a. Accounting reform
b. ABC Television Network
c. AMEX
d. AIG

35. The _____ is the national, professional association of CPAs in the United States, with more than 330,000 members, including CPAs in business and industry, public practice, government, and education; student affiliates; and international associates. It sets ethical standards for the profession and U.S. auditing standards for audits of private companies; federal, state and local governments; and non-profit organizations.

Approximately 40% of its members are engaged in the practice of public accounting, in areas such as auditing, accounting, taxation, general business consulting, business valuation, personal financial planning and business technology.

a. AIG
b. Other postemployment benefits
c. American Institute of Certified Public Accountants
d. ABC Television Network

36. _____ is the statutory title of qualified accountants in the United States who have passed the Uniform _____ Examination and have met additional state education and experience requirements for certification as a _____. Individuals who have passed the Exam but have not either accomplished the required on-the-job experience or have previously met it but in the meantime have lapsed their continuing professional education are, in many states, permitted the designation '_____ Inactive' or an equivalent phrase. In most U.S. states, only _____s who are licensed are able to provide to the public attestation (including auditing) opinions on financial statements.

a. Chartered Certified Accountant
b. Chartered Accountant
c. Certified General Accountant
d. Certified Public Accountant

37. The _____ is a private, not-for-profit organization whose primary purpose is to develop generally accepted accounting principles (GAAP) within the United States in the public's interest. The Securities and Exchange Commission (SEC) designated the _____ as the organization responsible for setting accounting standards for public companies in the U.S. It was created in 1973, replacing the Accounting Principles Board and the Committee on Accounting Procedure of the American Institute of Certified Public Accountants. The _____'s mission is 'to establish and improve standards of financial accounting and reporting for the guidance and education of the public, including issuers, auditors, and users of financial information.'

The _____ is not a governmental body.

  a. Governmental Accounting Standards Board
  b. Public company
  c. Privately held
  d. Financial Accounting Standards Board

38. _____ is the term used to refer to the standard framework of guidelines for financial accounting used in any given jurisdiction. _____ includes the standards, conventions, and rules accountants follow in recording and summarizing transactions, and in the preparation of financial statements.

Financial accounting information must be assembled and reported objectively.

  a. Current asset
  b. Long-term liabilities
  c. General ledger
  d. Generally accepted accounting principles

39. In economics, business, retail, and accounting, a _____ is the value of money that has been used up to produce something, and hence is not available for use anymore. In economics, a _____ is an alternative that is given up as a result of a decision. In business, the _____ may be one of acquisition, in which case the amount of money expended to acquire it is counted as _____.

  a. Cost of quality
  b. Prime cost
  c. Cost allocation
  d. Cost

40. The basic _____ is the foundation for the double-entry bookkeeping system. It shows how assets were financed: either by borrowing money from someone (liability) or by paying your own money (shareholders' equity.)

    Assets = Liabilities + (Shareholders or Owners equity)

For example: A student buys a computer for $945.

  a. Accounting equation
  b. AMEX
  c. AIG
  d. ABC Television Network

41. In business and accounting, _____ are everything of value that is owned by a person or company. It is a claim on the property your income of a borrower. The balance sheet of a firm records the monetary value of the _____ owned by the firm.

  a. Accounts receivable
  b. Assets
  c. Accrual basis accounting
  d. Earnings before interest, taxes, depreciation and amortization

Chapter 1. Introduction to Accounting and Business

42. In accounting, _____ are considered liabilities of the business that are to be settled in cash within the fiscal year or the operating cycle, whichever period is longer.

For example accounts payable for goods, services or supplies that were purchased for use in the operation of the business and payable within a normal period of time would be _____.

Bonds, mortgages and loans that are payable over a term exceeding one year would be fixed liabilities.

a. Payroll
b. Current Liabilities
c. Closing entries
d. Treasury stock

43. In accounting, _____ has a very specific meaning. It is an outflow of cash or other valuable assets from a person or company to another person or company. This outflow of cash is generally one side of a trade for products or services that have equal or better current or future value to the buyer than to the seller.

a. AIG
b. AMEX
c. Expense
d. ABC Television Network

44. _____ refers to services paid for in advance. Examples include tolls, pay as you go cell phones, and stored-value cards such as gift cards and preloaded credit cards. _____ accounts are assets, and they are increased by debiting the account(s.)

a. Prepaid
b. 3M Company
c. BMC Software, Inc.
d. BNSF Railway

45. _____, in accrual accounting, is any account where the asset or liability is not realized until a future date (accounting period), e.g. annuities, charges, taxes, income, etc. The _____ item may be carried, dependent on type of deferral, as either an asset or liability.

a. Pro forma
b. Payroll
c. Cash basis accounting
d. Deferred

46. A _____ is the pinnacle activity involved in selling products or services in return for money or other compensation. It is an act of completion of a commercial activity.

A _____ is completed by the seller, the owner of the goods.

a. Sale
b. Controlled Foreign Corporations
c. Serial bonds
d. Procter ' Gamble

47. _____ is a fee paid on borrowed assets. It is the price paid for the use of borrowed money, or, money earned by deposited funds. Assets that are sometimes lent with _____ include money, shares, consumer goods through hire purchase, major assets such as aircraft, and even entire factories in finance lease arrangements. The _____ is calculated upon the value of the assets in the same manner as upon money.

a. Interest
b. AIG
c. Insolvency
d. ABC Television Network

48. In finance, _____ is the interest that has accumulated since the principal investment, or since the previous interest payment if there has been one already. For a financial instrument such as a bond, interest is calculated and paid in set intervals.

The primary formula for calculating the interest accrued in a given period is:

$$I_A = T \times P \times R$$

where I_A is the _____, T is the fraction of the year, P is the principal, and R is the annualized interest rate.

a. AIG
c. Interest
b. ABC Television Network
d. Accrued interest

49. An _____, operating expenditure, operational expense, operational expenditure or OPEX is an on-going cost for running a product, business, or system. Its counterpart, a capital expenditure (CAPEX), is the cost of developing or providing non-consumable parts for the product or system. For example, the purchase of a photocopier is the CAPEX, and the annual paper and toner cost is the OPEX.

a. AMEX
c. Operating Expense
b. AIG
d. ABC Television Network

50. A _____ is the transfer of wealth from one party (such as a person or company) to another. A _____ is usually made in exchange for the provision of goods, services or both, or to fulfill a legal obligation.

The simplest and oldest form of _____ is barter, the exchange of one good or service for another.

a. Payment
c. 3M Company
b. Payee
d. BMC Software, Inc.

51. _____ are payments made by a corporation to its shareholder members. It is the portion of corporate profits paid out to stockholders. When a corporation earns a profit or surplus, that money can be put to two uses: it can either be re-invested in the business (called retained earnings), or it can be paid to the shareholders as a dividend.

a. Franking credit
c. Dividend payout ratio
b. Dividend stripping
d. Dividends

52. _____ is the balance of the amounts of cash being received and paid by a business during a defined period of time, sometimes tied to a specific project. Measurement of _____ can be used

- to evaluate the state or performance of a business or project.
- to determine problems with liquidity. Being profitable does not necessarily mean being liquid. A company can fail because of a shortage of cash, even while profitable.
- to project rate of returns. The time of _____s into and out of projects are used as inputs to financial models such as internal rate of return, and net present value.
- to examine income or growth of a business when it is believed that accrual accounting concepts do not represent economic realities. Alternately, _____ can be used to 'validate' the net income generated by accrual accounting.

Chapter 1. Introduction to Accounting and Business 11

_____ as a generic term may be used differently depending on context, and certain _____ definitions may be adapted by analysts and users for their own uses. Common terms include operating _____ and free _____.

- a. Gross profit
- b. Cash flow
- c. Flow-through entity
- d. Gross income

53. _____ is a specific term used in companies' financial reporting from the company-whole point of view. Because that use excludes the effects of changing ownership interest, an economic measure of _____ is necessary for financial analysis from the shareholders' point of view

_____ is defined by the Financial Accounting Standards Board, or FASB, as 'the change in equity [net assets] of a business enterprise during a period from transactions and other events and circumstances from nonowner sources. It includes all changes in equity during a period except those resulting from investments by owners and distributions to owners.'

_____ is the sum of net income and other items that must bypass the income statement because they have not been realized, including items like an unrealized holding gain or loss from available for sale securities and foreign currency translation gains or losses.

- a. 3M Company
- b. BNSF Railway
- c. BMC Software, Inc.
- d. Comprehensive income

54. _____ are formal records of a business' financial activities.

In British English, including United Kingdom company law, _____ are often referred to as accounts, although the term _____ is also used, particularly by accountants.

_____ provide an overview of a business' financial condition in both short and long term.

- a. Statement of retained earnings
- b. 3M Company
- c. Financial statements
- d. Notes to the financial statements

55. _____ are financial statements that factor the holding company's subsidiaries into its aggregated accounting figure. It is a representation of how the holding company is doing as a group. The consolidated accounts should provide a true and fair view of the financial and operating conditions of the group.

- a. Replacement cost
- b. Committee on Accounting Procedure
- c. Redemption value
- d. Consolidated financial statements

56. In cost-volume-profit analysis, a form of management accounting, _____ is the marginal profit per unit sale. It is a useful quantity in carrying out various calculations, and can be used as a measure of operating leverage.

The Total _____ is Total Revenue (TR, or Sales) minus Total Variable Cost (TVC):

   Tcontribution margin = TR − TVC

The Unit _____ (C) is Unit Revenue (Price, P) minus Unit Variable Cost (V):

   C = P − V

The _____ Ratio is the percentage of Contribution over Total Revenue, which can be calculated from the unit contribution over unit price or total contribution over Total Revenue:

$$\frac{C}{P} = \frac{P-V}{P} = \frac{\text{Unit Contribution Margin}}{\text{Price}} = \frac{\text{Total Contribution Margin}}{\text{Total Revenue}}$$

For instance, if the price is $10 and the unit variable cost is $2, then the unit _____ is $8, and the _____ ratio is $8/$10 = 80%.

   a. Profit center
   c. Cost driver
   b. Factory overhead
   d. Contribution margin

57. _____ is a company's financial statement that indicates how the revenue is transformed into the net income The purpose of the _____ is to show managers and investors whether the company made or lost money during the period being reported.

The important thing to remember about an _____ is that it represents a period of time.

   a. ABC Television Network
   c. AMEX
   b. Income statement
   d. AIG

58. _____ is equal to the income that a firm has after subtracting costs and expenses from the total revenue. _____ can be distributed among holders of common stock as a dividend or held by the firm as retained earnings.

The items deducted will typically include tax expense, financing expense (interest expense), and minority interest. Likewise, preferred stock dividends will be subtracted too, though they are not an expense.

   a. Net income
   c. Matching principle
   b. Generally accepted accounting principles
   d. Long-term liabilities

59. In business and finance accounting, _____ is equal to the gross profit minus overheads minus interest payable plus/minus one off items for a given time period (usually: accounting period.)

A common synonym for '_____' when discussing financial statements (which include a balance sheet and an income statement) is the bottom line. This term results from the traditional appearance of an income statement which shows all allocated revenues and expenses over a specified time period with the resulting summation on the bottom line of the report.

    a. Salvage value
    b. Cost of goods sold
    c. Treasury stock
    d. Net profit

60. A _____ is a computer application that simulates a paper worksheet. It displays multiple cells that together make up a grid consisting of rows and columns, each cell containing either alphanumeric text or numeric values. A _____ cell may alternatively contain a formula that defines how the contents of that cell is to be calculated from the contents of any other cell (or combination of cells) each time any cell is updated.

    a. Merck ' Co., Inc.
    b. Linear regression
    c. Mutual fund
    d. Spreadsheet

61. In financial accounting, a _____ or Statement of cash flows is a financial statement that shows a company's flow of cash. The money coming into the business is called cash inflow, and money going out from the business is called cash outflow. The statement shows how changes in balance sheet and income accounts affect cash and cash equivalents, and breaks the analysis down to operating, investing, and financing activities.

    a. 3M Company
    b. BMC Software, Inc.
    c. BNSF Railway
    d. Cash flow statement

Chapter 2. Analyzing Transactions

1. _____ and credit are formal bookkeeping and accounting terms. They are the most fundamental concepts in accounting, representing the two records that one party in a transaction makes on its records, transferring a money balance from one account to another, one representing a reduction of liability or increase in asset, and the other representing a balancing increase in liability or reduction of asset.

Introduction

_____s and credits are a system of notation used in accounting to keep track of money movements (transactions) into and out of an account.

   a. Double-entry bookkeeping
   b. Bookkeeping
   c. Cookie jar accounting
   d. Debit

2. The term _____, derived from the distinctive T shape, is frequently used when discussing or analyzing accounting or business transactions. _____s are used to represent general ledger accounts.

Typically one or more Ts are drawn on a white board or blank piece of paper. A general ledger account name or number is then written above each T. Debit entries are recorded on the left side of the 'T' and credit entries are recorded on the right side of the 'T'.

   a. 3M Company
   b. BNSF Railway
   c. BMC Software, Inc.
   d. T account

3. In business and accounting, _____ are everything of value that is owned by a person or company. It is a claim on the property your income of a borrower. The balance sheet of a firm records the monetary value of the _____ owned by the firm.
   a. Earnings before interest, taxes, depreciation and amortization
   b. Accounts receivable
   c. Accrual basis accounting
   d. Assets

4. _____ is a list of the accounts including a unique number of each allowing to locate it in each ledger. The list is typically arranged in the order of the customary appearance of accounts in the financial statements. A _____ can track a specific financial information.
   a. Journal entry
   b. General ledger
   c. General journal
   d. Chart of accounts

5. _____ are payments made by a corporation to its shareholder members. It is the portion of corporate profits paid out to stockholders. When a corporation earns a profit or surplus, that money can be put to two uses: it can either be re-invested in the business (called retained earnings), or it can be paid to the shareholders as a dividend.
   a. Dividends
   b. Dividend payout ratio
   c. Dividend stripping
   d. Franking credit

6. In accounting, _____ has a very specific meaning. It is an outflow of cash or other valuable assets from a person or company to another person or company. This outflow of cash is generally one side of a trade for products or services that have equal or better current or future value to the buyer than to the seller.

a. AMEX
b. AIG
c. ABC Television Network
d. Expense

7. _____ is a process by which a firm can obtain the use of a certain fixed assets for which it must pay a series of contractual, periodic, tax deductable payments. The lessee is the receiver of the services or the assets under the lease contract and the lessor is the owner of the assets. The relationship between the tenant and the landlord is called a tenancy, and can be for a fixed or an indefinite period of time (called the term of the lease.)
 a. Due diligence
 b. Leasing
 c. Tax lien
 d. Limited liability

8. In financial accounting, a _____ is defined as an obligation of an entity arising from past transactions or events, the settlement of which may result in the transfer or use of assets, provision of services or other yielding of economic benefits in the future.
 a. Pre-emption right
 b. Liability
 c. Trust Indenture Act of 1939
 d. Resource Conservation and Recovery Act

9. _____, in accrual accounting, (e.g. advance payment received from a client) is, according to revenue recognition, revenue not earned until the delivery of goods or services, which until then, is still owed to the payer, hence remaining a liability.

_____, sometimes referred to as deferred revenue or unearned revenue, shares characteristics with accrued expense with the difference that a liability to be covered latter is cash received FROM a counterpart, while goods or services are to be delivered in a latter period, when such income item is earned, the related revenue item is recognized, and the same amount is deducted from deferred revenues.

 a. Treasury stock
 b. Gross sales
 c. Matching principle
 d. Deferred income

10. _____ is the balance of the amounts of cash being received and paid by a business during a defined period of time, sometimes tied to a specific project. Measurement of _____ can be used

- to evaluate the state or performance of a business or project.
- to determine problems with liquidity. Being profitable does not necessarily mean being liquid. A company can fail because of a shortage of cash, even while profitable.
- to project rate of returns. The time of _____s into and out of projects are used as inputs to financial models such as internal rate of return, and net present value.
- to examine income or growth of a business when it is believed that accrual accounting concepts do not represent economic realities. Alternately, _____ can be used to 'validate' the net income generated by accrual accounting.

_____ as a generic term may be used differently depending on context, and certain _____ definitions may be adapted by analysts and users for their own uses. Common terms include operating _____ and free _____.

 a. Flow-through entity
 b. Gross income
 c. Gross profit
 d. Cash flow

11. In accounting, _____ are considered liabilities of the business that are to be settled in cash within the fiscal year or the operating cycle, whichever period is longer.

For example accounts payable for goods, services or supplies that were purchased for use in the operation of the business and payable within a normal period of time would be _____.

Bonds, mortgages and loans that are payable over a term exceeding one year would be fixed liabilities.

a. Closing entries
b. Payroll
c. Treasury stock
d. Current Liabilities

12. A _____, also client, buyer or purchaser is the buyer or user of the paid products of an individual or organization, mostly called the supplier or seller. This is typically through purchasing or renting goods or services.

a. BMC Software, Inc.
b. 3M Company
c. BNSF Railway
d. Customer

13. _____, also known as property, plant, and equipment (PP&E), is a term used in accountancy for assets and property which cannot easily be converted into cash. This can be compared with current assets such as cash or bank accounts, which are described as liquid assets. In most cases, only tangible assets are referred to as fixed.

a. Certified Practising Accountant
b. Remittance advice
c. Lower of Cost or Market
d. Fixed asset

14. An _____, operating expenditure, operational expense, operational expenditure or OPEX is an on-going cost for running a product, business, or system. Its counterpart, a capital expenditure (CAPEX), is the cost of developing or providing non-consumable parts for the product or system. For example, the purchase of a photocopier is the CAPEX, and the annual paper and toner cost is the OPEX.

a. AMEX
b. AIG
c. ABC Television Network
d. Operating Expense

15. A _____ is the transfer of wealth from one party (such as a person or company) to another. A _____ is usually made in exchange for the provision of goods, services or both, or to fulfill a legal obligation.

The simplest and oldest form of _____ is barter, the exchange of one good or service for another.

a. Payee
b. BMC Software, Inc.
c. Payment
d. 3M Company

16. In financial accounting, a _____ or statement of financial position is a summary of a person's or organization's balances. Assets, liabilities and ownership equity are listed as of a specific date, such as the end of its financial year. A _____ is often described as a snapshot of a company's financial condition.

a. 3M Company
b. Notes to the financial statements
c. Statement of retained earnings
d. Balance sheet

17. A _____ has several related meanings:

- a daily record of events or business; a private _____ is usually referred to as a diary.
- a newspaper or other periodical, in the literal sense of one published each day;
- many publications issued at stated intervals, such as magazines, or scholarly academic _____s, or the record of the transactions of a society, are often called _____s. Although _____ is sometimes used, erroneously, as a synonym for 'magazine,' in academic use, a _____ refers to a serious, scholarly publication, most often peer-reviewed. A non-scholarly magazine written for an educated audience about an industry or an area of professional activity is usually called a professional magazine.

The word 'journalist' for one whose business is writing for the public press has been in use since the end of the 17th century.

Open access _____s are scholarly _____s that are available to the reader without financial or other barrier other than access to the internet itself. Some are subsidized, and some require payment on behalf of the author. Subsidized _____s are financed by an academic institution or a government information center.

a. BNSF Railway
b. BMC Software, Inc.
c. 3M Company
d. Journal

18. A _____, in accounting, is a logging of transcriptions into items accounting journal. The _____ can consist of several items, each of which is either a debit or a credit. The total of the debits must equal the total of the credits, or the _____ is said to be 'unbalanced.' Journal entries can record unique items or recurring items such as depreciation or bond amortization.

a. Sales journal
b. General journal
c. General ledger
d. Journal entry

19. In accounting/accountancy, _____ are journal entries usually made at the end of an accounting period to allocate income and expenditure to the period in which they actually occurred. The revenue recognition principle is the basis of making _____ that pertain to unearned and accrued revenues under accrual-basis accounting. They are sometimes called Balance Day adjustments because they are made on balance day.

a. Accrued expense
b. Earnings before interest, taxes, depreciation and amortization
c. Adjusting entries
d. Accrual

20. _____ are journal entries made at the end of an accounting period to transfer temporary accounts to permanent accounts. An 'income summary' account may be used to show the balance between revenue and expenses, or they could be directly closed against retained earnings where dividend payments will be deducted from. This process is used to reset the balance of these temporary accounts to zero for the next accounting period.

a. Treasury stock
b. Closing entries
c. Trial balance
d. FIFO and LIFO accounting

21. _____ is a company's financial statement that indicates how the revenue is transformed into the net income The purpose of the _____ is to show managers and investors whether the company made or lost money during the period being reported.

The important thing to remember about an _____ is that it represents a period of time.

a. ABC Television Network
c. AMEX
b. AIG
d. Income statement

22. The basic _____ is the foundation for the double-entry bookkeeping system. It shows how assets were financed: either by borrowing money from someone (liability) or by paying your own money (shareholders' equity.)

Assets = Liabilities + (Shareholders or Owners equity)

For example: A student buys a computer for $945.

a. ABC Television Network
c. Accounting equation
b. AMEX
d. AIG

23. _____ is a system of financial accounting where each transaction is recorded in at least two accounts: at least one account is debited and at least one account is credited, so that the total debits of the transaction equal to the total credits. For example, if Company A sells an item to Company B, and Company B pays by cheque, then the bookkeeper of Company A credits the account 'Sales' and debits the account 'Bank'. Conversely, the bookkeeper of Company B debits the account 'Purchases' and credits the account 'Bank'.

a. Debit and credit
c. Controlling account
b. Bookkeeping
d. Double-entry bookkeeping

24. In economics, business, retail, and accounting, a _____ is the value of money that has been used up to produce something, and hence is not available for use anymore. In economics, a _____ is an alternative that is given up as a result of a decision. In business, the _____ may be one of acquisition, in which case the amount of money expended to acquire it is counted as _____.

a. Prime cost
c. Cost allocation
b. Cost
d. Cost of quality

25. _____ are formal bookkeeping and accounting terms. They are the most fundamental concepts in accounting, representing the two records that one party in a transaction makes on its records, transferring a money balance from one account to another, one representing a reduction of liability or increase in asset, and the other representing a balancing increase in liability or reduction of asset.

Debits and credits are a system of notation used in accounting to keep track of money movements (transactions) into and out of an account.

a. Double-entry bookkeeping
c. Bookkeeping
b. Controlling account
d. Debit and credit

26. In accounting, the _____ is a worksheet listing the balance at a certain date, of each ledger account in two columns, namely debit and credit. Under the double-entry system, in any transaction the total of any debits must equal the total of any credits, so in a _____ the total of the debit side should always be equal to the total of the credit side. The _____ thus serves as a tool to detect errors, which can result in the totals not being equal.

a. Bottom line
b. Depreciation
c. Current asset
d. Trial balance

Chapter 3. The Adjusting Process

1. An _____ is a period with reference to which United Kingdom corporation tax is charged. It helps dictate when tax is paid on income and gains. An _____ begins whenever a company comes within the corporation tax charge, and whenever an _____ ends without the company ceasing to be within the charge.
   a. Accounting period
   b. ABC Television Network
   c. AIG
   d. AMEX

2. _____ of something is, in finance, the adding together of interest or different investments over a period of time such as atoms (1 - the act or process of accruing; 2 - the amount that accrues.) It holds specific meanings in accounting and payroll.

   _____, in accounting, describes the accounting method known as _____ basis, whereby revenues and expenses are recognized when they are accrued, i.e. accumulated (earned or incurred), regardless when the actual cash is received or paid out.
   a. Assets
   b. Accounts receivable
   c. Earnings before interest, taxes, depreciation and amortization
   d. Accrual

3. _____ is a method of accounting whereby economic activities (rather than cash flow) of financial events are considered, because of two complementary principles, which (together) determine the point, at which expenses and revenues are recognized. According to revenue recognition principle, revenues are realized when earned, whether or not they are received in cash.
   a. Accrual
   b. Accrual basis accounting
   c. Earnings before interest, taxes, depreciation and amortization
   d. Accrued revenue

4. _____ is a cornerstone of accrual accounting together with the revenue recognition principle. They both determine the accounting period, in which revenues and expenses are recognized. According to the principle, expenses are recognized when obligations are (1) incurred (usually when goods are transferred or services rendered, e.g. sold), and (2) offset against recognized revenues, which were generated from those expenses (related on the cause-and-effect basis), no matter when cash is paid out.
   a. Matching principle
   b. Net sales
   c. Current liabilities
   d. Payroll

5. _____ principle is a cornerstone of accrual accounting together with matching principle. They both determine the accounting period, in which revenues and expenses are recognized. According to the principle, revenues are recognized when they are (1) realized or realizable, and are (2) earned (usually when goods are transferred or services rendered), no matter when cash is received.
   a. Revenue recognition
   b. BMC Software, Inc.
   c. Net realizable value
   d. 3M Company

6. In accounting/accountancy, _____ are journal entries usually made at the end of an accounting period to allocate income and expenditure to the period in which they actually occurred. The revenue recognition principle is the basis of making _____ that pertain to unearned and accrued revenues under accrual-basis accounting. They are sometimes called Balance Day adjustments because they are made on balance day.

a. Adjusting entries
b. Accrual
c. Earnings before interest, taxes, depreciation and amortization
d. Accrued expense

7. _____ is an asset, such as unpaid proceeds from a delivery of goods or services, at which such income item is earned and the related revenue item is recognized, while cash for them is to be received in a latter period, when its amount is deducted from the _____.
   a. Accrued expense
   b. Accounts receivable
   c. Assets
   d. Accrued revenue

8. In accounting, _____ has a very specific meaning. It is an outflow of cash or other valuable assets from a person or company to another person or company. This outflow of cash is generally one side of a trade for products or services that have equal or better current or future value to the buyer than to the seller.
   a. ABC Television Network
   b. AIG
   c. AMEX
   d. Expense

9. _____, is a liability with an uncertain timing or amount, but where the uncertainty is not significant enough to qualify it as a provision. An example is an unpaid obligation to pay for goods or services received FROM a counterpart, while cash for them is to be paid out in a latter accounting period when its amount is deducted from _____s.
   a. Accounts receivable
   b. Assets
   c. Accrual basis accounting
   d. Accrued expense

10. _____ are liabilities which have occurred, but have not been paid or logged under accounts payable during an accounting period; in other words, obligations for goods and services provided to a company for which invoices have not yet been received. Examples would include accrued wages payable, accrued sales tax payable, and accrued rent payable.

There are two general types of _____:

- Routine and recurring
- Infrequent or non-routine

Most companies pay their employees on a predetermined schedule. Let's say that the 'Imaginary company Ltd.' pays its employees each Friday for the hours worked that week.

   a. ABC Television Network
   b. Accrued liabilities
   c. AMEX
   d. AIG

11. In business and accounting, _____ are everything of value that is owned by a person or company. It is a claim on the property your income of a borrower. The balance sheet of a firm records the monetary value of the _____ owned by the firm.
   a. Assets
   b. Accrual basis accounting
   c. Earnings before interest, taxes, depreciation and amortization
   d. Accounts receivable

12. _____, in accrual accounting, is any account where the asset or liability is not realized until a future date (accounting period), e.g. annuities, charges, taxes, income, etc. The _____ item may be carried, dependent on type of deferral, as either an asset or liability.
    a. Payroll
    b. Cash basis accounting
    c. Pro forma
    d. Deferred

13. _____, in accrual accounting, (e.g. advance payment received from a client) is, according to revenue recognition, revenue not earned until the delivery of goods or services, which until then, is still owed to the payer, hence remaining a liability.

    _____, sometimes referred to as deferred revenue or unearned revenue, shares characteristics with accrued expense with the difference that a liability to be covered latter is cash received FROM a counterpart, while goods or services are to be delivered in a latter period, when such income item is earned, the related revenue item is recognized, and the same amount is deducted from deferred revenues.

    a. Deferred income
    b. Gross sales
    c. Matching principle
    d. Treasury stock

14. In financial accounting, a _____ is defined as an obligation of an entity arising from past transactions or events, the settlement of which may result in the transfer or use of assets, provision of services or other yielding of economic benefits in the future.
    a. Resource Conservation and Recovery Act
    b. Trust Indenture Act of 1939
    c. Pre-emption right
    d. Liability

15. _____ refers to services paid for in advance. Examples include tolls, pay as you go cell phones, and stored-value cards such as gift cards and preloaded credit cards. _____ accounts are assets, and they are increased by debiting the account(s.)
    a. BNSF Railway
    b. BMC Software, Inc.
    c. 3M Company
    d. Prepaid

16. _____ is a list of the accounts including a unique number of each allowing to locate it in each ledger. The list is typically arranged in the order of the customary appearance of accounts in the financial statements. A _____ can track a specific financial information.
    a. General ledger
    b. Journal entry
    c. General journal
    d. Chart of accounts

17. _____ is the generic term that refers to all supplies regularly used in offices by businesses and other organizations, from private citizens to governments, who works with the collection, refinement, and output of information (colloquially referred to as 'paper work'.) _____ being sold at a drugstore. Hà Ná»™i's Stationery supplier

The term includes small, expendable, daily use items such as paper clips, staples, hole punches, binders and laminators, writing utensils and paper, but also encompasses higher-cost equipment like computers, printers, fax machines, photocopiers and cash registers, as well as office furniture such as cubicles or armoire desks. Two very common medium-to-high-cost office equipment items before the advent of suitably priced word processing machines and PCs in the 1970s and 1980s were typewriters and adding machines.

Chapter 3. The Adjusting Process

    a. Office supplies
    b. ABC Television Network
    c. AMEX
    d. AIG

18. A _____ is a compensation, usually financial, received by a worker in exchange for their labor.

Compensation in terms of _____s is given to worker and compensation in terms of salary is given to employees. Compensation is a monetary benefits given to employees in returns of the services provided by them.

    a. BMC Software, Inc.
    b. 3M Company
    c. Retirement plan
    d. Wage

19. Book Value = Original Cost - _____

Book value at the end of year becomes book value at the beginning of next year. The asset is depreciated until the book value equals scrap value.

If the vehicle were to be sold and the sales price exceeded the depreciated value (net book value) then the excess would be considered a gain and subject to depreciation recapture.

    a. AMEX
    b. AIG
    c. ABC Television Network
    d. Accumulated depreciation

20. In accounting, _____ or carrying value is the value of an asset according to its balance sheet account balance. For assets, the value is based on the original cost of the asset less any depreciation, amortization or impairment costs made against the asset. Traditionally, a company's _____ is its total assets minus intangible assets and liabilities.

    a. Generally accepted accounting principles
    b. Matching principle
    c. Book value
    d. Depreciation

21. _____ are formal bookkeeping and accounting terms. They are the most fundamental concepts in accounting, representing the two records that one party in a transaction makes on its records, transferring a money balance from one account to another, one representing a reduction of liability or increase in asset, and the other representing a balancing increase in liability or reduction of asset.

Debits and credits are a system of notation used in accounting to keep track of money movements (transactions) into and out of an account.

    a. Double-entry bookkeeping
    b. Controlling account
    c. Debit and credit
    d. Bookkeeping

22. _____ is a term used in accounting, economics and finance to spread the cost of an asset over the span of several years.

In simple words we can say that _____ is the reduction in the value of an asset due to usage, passage of time, wear and tear, technological outdating or obsolescence, depletion, inadequacy, rot, rust, decay or other such factors.

Chapter 3. The Adjusting Process

In accounting, _____ is a term used to describe any method of attributing the historical or purchase cost of an asset across its useful life, roughly corresponding to normal wear and tear.

- a. Net profit
- b. Current asset
- c. General ledger
- d. Depreciation

23. _____, also known as property, plant, and equipment (PP&E), is a term used in accountancy for assets and property which cannot easily be converted into cash. This can be compared with current assets such as cash or bank accounts, which are described as liquid assets. In most cases, only tangible assets are referred to as fixed.

- a. Remittance advice
- b. Certified Practising Accountant
- c. Fixed asset
- d. Lower of Cost or Market

24. In economics, business, retail, and accounting, a _____ is the value of money that has been used up to produce something, and hence is not available for use anymore. In economics, a _____ is an alternative that is given up as a result of a decision. In business, the _____ may be one of acquisition, in which case the amount of money expended to acquire it is counted as _____.

- a. Cost allocation
- b. Cost of quality
- c. Prime cost
- d. Cost

25. In finance, _____ is the process of estimating the potential market value of a financial asset or liability. They can be done on assets (for example, investments in marketable securities such as stocks, options, business enterprises, or intangible assets such as patents and trademarks) or on liabilities (e.g., Bonds issued by a company.) A _____ is required in many contexts including investment analysis, capital budgeting, merger and acquisition transactions, financial reporting, taxable events to determine the proper tax liability, and in litigation.

- a. Daybook
- b. Capital
- c. Pay-as-you-go
- d. Valuation

26. _____ is a process by which a firm can obtain the use of a certain fixed assets for which it must pay a series of contractual, periodic, tax deductable payments. The lessee is the receiver of the services or the assets under the lease contract and the lessor is the owner of the assets. The relationship between the tenant and the landlord is called a tenancy, and can be for a fixed or an indefinite period of time (called the term of the lease.)

- a. Leasing
- b. Tax lien
- c. Limited liability
- d. Due diligence

27. In accounting, the _____ is a worksheet listing the balance at a certain date, of each ledger account in two columns, namely debit and credit. Under the double-entry system, in any transaction the total of any debits must equal the total of any credits, so in a _____ the total of the debit side should always be equal to the total of the credit side. The _____ thus serves as a tool to detect errors, which can result in the totals not being equal.

- a. Depreciation
- b. Current asset
- c. Bottom line
- d. Trial balance

Chapter 4. Completing the Accounting Cycle

1. _____ are formal records of a business' financial activities.

In British English, including United Kingdom company law, _____ are often referred to as accounts, although the term _____ is also used, particularly by accountants.

_____ provide an overview of a business' financial condition in both short and long term.

   a. Statement of retained earnings   b. Financial statements
   c. 3M Company   d. Notes to the financial statements

2. _____ is a company's financial statement that indicates how the revenue is transformed into the net income The purpose of the _____ is to show managers and investors whether the company made or lost money during the period being reported.

The important thing to remember about an _____ is that it represents a period of time.

   a. AMEX   b. ABC Television Network
   c. AIG   d. Income statement

3. _____ is a specific term used in companies' financial reporting from the company-whole point of view. Because that use excludes the effects of changing ownership interest, an economic measure of _____ is necessary for financial analysis from the shareholders' point of view

_____ is defined by the Financial Accounting Standards Board, or FASB, as 'the change in equity [net assets] of a business enterprise during a period from transactions and other events and circumstances from nonowner sources. It includes all changes in equity during a period except those resulting from investments by owners and distributions to owners.'

_____ is the sum of net income and other items that must bypass the income statement because they have not been realized, including items like an unrealized holding gain or loss from available for sale securities and foreign currency translation gains or losses.

   a. 3M Company   b. BMC Software, Inc.
   c. Comprehensive income   d. BNSF Railway

4. _____ is defined by The Wall Street Journal, as a form of barter that involves a company selling 'an unused asset to another company while at the same time agreeing to buy back the same or similar assets at about the same price.' Round trips are characteristic of the New Economy companies. They played a crucial part in temporarily inflating the market capitalization of energy traders such as Enron, CMS Energy, Reliant Energy, and Dynegy.

Other companies making unconventional _____ deals include AOL with Sun Microsystems and Global Crossing with Qwest Communications.

   a. Net pay   b. Residual value
   c. 3M Company   d. Round-tripping

5. In business and accounting, _____ are everything of value that is owned by a person or company. It is a claim on the property your income of a borrower. The balance sheet of a firm records the monetary value of the _____ owned by the firm.

   a. Accounts receivable
   b. Earnings before interest, taxes, depreciation and amortization
   c. Accrual basis accounting
   d. Assets

6. In financial accounting, a _____ or statement of financial position is a summary of a person's or organization's balances. Assets, liabilities and ownership equity are listed as of a specific date, such as the end of its financial year. A _____ is often described as a snapshot of a company's financial condition.

   a. Statement of retained earnings
   b. Notes to the financial statements
   c. 3M Company
   d. Balance sheet

7. In accounting, a _____ is an asset on the balance sheet which is expected to be sold or otherwise used up in the near future, usually within one year, or one business cycle - whichever is longer. Typical _____s include cash, cash equivalents, accounts receivable, inventory, the portion of prepaid accounts which will be used within a year, and short-term investments.

On the balance sheet, assets will typically be classified into _____s and long-term assets.

   a. Deferred
   b. Pro forma
   c. General ledger
   d. Current asset

8. In accounting, _____ are considered liabilities of the business that are to be settled in cash within the fiscal year or the operating cycle, whichever period is longer.

For example accounts payable for goods, services or supplies that were purchased for use in the operation of the business and payable within a normal period of time would be _____.

Bonds, mortgages and loans that are payable over a term exceeding one year would be fixed liabilities.

   a. Payroll
   b. Closing entries
   c. Treasury stock
   d. Current liabilities

9. _____, also known as property, plant, and equipment (PP&E), is a term used in accountancy for assets and property which cannot easily be converted into cash. This can be compared with current assets such as cash or bank accounts, which are described as liquid assets. In most cases, only tangible assets are referred to as fixed.

   a. Certified Practising Accountant
   b. Remittance advice
   c. Lower of Cost or Market
   d. Fixed asset

10. In financial accounting, a _____ is defined as an obligation of an entity arising from past transactions or events, the settlement of which may result in the transfer or use of assets, provision of services or other yielding of economic benefits in the future.

   a. Pre-emption right
   b. Trust Indenture Act of 1939
   c. Resource Conservation and Recovery Act
   d. Liability

Chapter 4. Completing the Accounting Cycle

11. In economic models, the _____ time frame assumes no fixed factors of production. Firms can enter or leave the marketplace, and the cost (and availability) of land, labor, raw materials, and capital goods can be assumed to vary. In contrast, in the short-run time frame, certain factors are assumed to be fixed, because there is not sufficient time for them to change.
    a. Short-run
    b. 3M Company
    c. BMC Software, Inc.
    d. Long-run

12. _____ are liabilities with a future benefit over one year, such as notes payable that mature greater than one year.

In accounting, the _____ are shown on the right wing of the balance-sheet representing the sources of funds, which are generally bounded in form of capital assets.

Examples of _____ are debentures, mortgage loans and other bank loans (note: not all bank loans are long term as not all are paid over a period greater than a year, the example is bridging loan.)
    a. Gross sales
    b. Cash basis accounting
    c. Book value
    d. Long-term liabilities

13. _____ represents claims for which formal instruments of credit are issued as evidence of debt, such as a promissory note. The credit instrument normally requires the debtor to pay interest and extends for time periods of 60-90 days or longer.
    a. Restricted stock
    b. Public offering
    c. Notes receivable
    d. Moving average

14. _____ is any physical or virtual entity that is owned by an individual or jointly by a group of individuals. An owner of _____ has the right to consume, sell, rent, mortgage, transfer and exchange his or her _____. Important widely-recognized types of _____ include real _____, personal _____ (other physical possessions), and intellectual _____ (rights over artistic creations, inventions, etc.), although the latter is not always as widely recognized or enforced.
    a. Limited liability
    b. Board of directors
    c. Corporate governance
    d. Property

15. _____ is a file or account that contains money that a person or company owes to suppliers, but has not paid yet (a form of debt.) When you receive an invoice you add it to the file, and then you remove it when you pay. Thus, the A/P is a form of credit that suppliers offer to their purchasers by allowing them to pay for a product or service after it has already been received.
    a. Accounts payable
    b. Earnings before interest, taxes, depreciation and amortization
    c. Accrual
    d. Accounts receivable

16. In economics, business, retail, and accounting, a _____ is the value of money that has been used up to produce something, and hence is not available for use anymore. In economics, a _____ is an alternative that is given up as a result of a decision. In business, the _____ may be one of acquisition, in which case the amount of money expended to acquire it is counted as _____.
    a. Cost allocation
    b. Cost of quality
    c. Prime cost
    d. Cost

17. _____ are journal entries made at the end of an accounting period to transfer temporary accounts to permanent accounts. An 'income summary' account may be used to show the balance between revenue and expenses, or they could be directly closed against retained earnings where dividend payments will be deducted from. This process is used to reset the balance of these temporary accounts to zero for the next accounting period.
   a. Treasury stock
   b. FIFO and LIFO accounting
   c. Trial balance
   d. Closing entries

18. A _____ is the transfer of an interest in property (or the equivalent in law - a charge) to a lender as a security for a debt - usually a loan of money. While a _____ in itself is not a debt, it is the lender's security for a debt. It is a transfer of an interest in land (or the equivalent) from the owner to the _____ lender, on the condition that this interest will be returned to the owner when the terms of the _____ have been satisfied or performed.
   a. BMC Software, Inc.
   b. BNSF Railway
   c. 3M Company
   d. Mortgage

19. A _____, also referred to as a note payable in accounting, is a contract where one party (the maker or issuer) makes an unconditional promise in writing to pay a sum of money to the other (the payee), either at a fixed or determinable future time or on demand of the payee, under specific terms. They differ from IOUs in that they contain a specific promise to pay, rather than simply acknowledging that a debt exists.

The terms of a note typically include the principal amount, the interest rate if any, and the maturity date.

   a. BNSF Railway
   b. BMC Software, Inc.
   c. 3M Company
   d. Promissory note

20. A _____ is usually a temporary account containing costs or amounts that are to be transferred to another account. An example is the income summary account containing revenue and expense amounts to be transferred to retained earnings at the close of a fiscal period.
   a. Special assessment
   b. Tax Analysts
   c. Clearing account
   d. Malcolm Baldrige National Quality Award

21. A _____ is a common type of chart, that represents an algorithm or process, showing the steps as boxes of various kinds, and their order by connecting these with arrows. _____s are used in analyzing, designing, documenting or managing a process or program in various fields.

The first structured method for documenting process flow, the 'flow process chart', was introduced by Frank Gilbreth to members of ASME in 1921 as the presentation e;Process Charts--First Steps in Finding the One Best Waye;.

   a. BMC Software, Inc.
   b. 3M Company
   c. BNSF Railway
   d. Flowchart

22. In accounting/accountancy, _____ are journal entries usually made at the end of an accounting period to allocate income and expenditure to the period in which they actually occurred. The revenue recognition principle is the basis of making _____ that pertain to unearned and accrued revenues under accrual-basis accounting. They are sometimes called Balance Day adjustments because they are made on balance day.

a. Earnings before interest, taxes, depreciation and amortization
b. Accrued expense
c. Accrual
d. Adjusting entries

23. In accounting, the _____ is a worksheet listing the balance at a certain date, of each ledger account in two columns, namely debit and credit. Under the double-entry system, in any transaction the total of any debits must equal the total of any credits, so in a _____ the total of the debit side should always be equal to the total of the credit side. The _____ thus serves as a tool to detect errors, which can result in the totals not being equal.

   a. Depreciation
   b. Trial balance
   c. Current asset
   d. Bottom line

24. An _____ invented by esteemed professor Karen Osterheld is the system of records a business keeps to maintain its accounting system. This includes the purchase, sales, and other financial processes of the business. The purpose of an _____ is to accumulate data and provide decision makers (investors, creditors, and managers) with information to make decision While this was previously a paper-based process, most modern businesses now use accounting software such as UBS, MYOB etc.

   a. AIG
   b. Accounting information system
   c. ABC Television Network
   d. AMEX

25. A _____ has several related meanings:

   - a daily record of events or business; a private _____ is usually referred to as a diary.
   - a newspaper or other periodical, in the literal sense of one published each day;
   - many publications issued at stated intervals, such as magazines, or scholarly academic _____s, or the record of the transactions of a society, are often called _____s. Although _____ is sometimes used, erroneously, as a synonym for 'magazine,' in academic use, a _____ refers to a serious, scholarly publication, most often peer-reviewed. A non-scholarly magazine written for an educated audience about an industry or an area of professional activity is usually called a professional magazine.

The word 'journalist' for one whose business is writing for the public press has been in use since the end of the 17th century.

Open access _____s are scholarly _____s that are available to the reader without financial or other barrier other than access to the internet itself. Some are subsidized, and some require payment on behalf of the author. Subsidized _____s are financed by an academic institution or a government information center.

   a. BNSF Railway
   b. BMC Software, Inc.
   c. 3M Company
   d. Journal

26. _____ is a process by which a firm can obtain the use of a certain fixed assets for which it must pay a series of contractual, periodic, tax deductable payments. The lessee is the receiver of the services or the assets under the lease contract and the lessor is the owner of the assets. The relationship between the tenant and the landlord is called a tenancy, and can be for a fixed or an indefinite period of time (called the term of the lease.)

   a. Tax lien
   b. Due diligence
   c. Limited liability
   d. Leasing

Chapter 4. Completing the Accounting Cycle

27. _____ is the balance of the amounts of cash being received and paid by a business during a defined period of time, sometimes tied to a specific project. Measurement of _____ can be used

- to evaluate the state or performance of a business or project.
- to determine problems with liquidity. Being profitable does not necessarily mean being liquid. A company can fail because of a shortage of cash, even while profitable.
- to project rate of returns. The time of _____s into and out of projects are used as inputs to financial models such as internal rate of return, and net present value.
- to examine income or growth of a business when it is believed that accrual accounting concepts do not represent economic realities. Alternately, _____ can be used to 'validate' the net income generated by accrual accounting.

_____ as a generic term may be used differently depending on context, and certain _____ definitions may be adapted by analysts and users for their own uses. Common terms include operating _____ and free _____.

a. Cash flow
c. Gross profit
b. Flow-through entity
d. Gross income

28. A _____ is a computer application that simulates a paper worksheet. It displays multiple cells that together make up a grid consisting of rows and columns, each cell containing either alphanumeric text or numeric values. A _____ cell may alternatively contain a formula that defines how the contents of that cell is to be calculated from the contents of any other cell (or combination of cells) each time any cell is updated.

a. Spreadsheet
c. Merck ' Co., Inc.
b. Linear regression
d. Mutual fund

29. In financial accounting, a _____ or Statement of cash flows is a financial statement that shows a company's flow of cash. The money coming into the business is called cash inflow, and money going out from the business is called cash outflow. The statement shows how changes in balance sheet and income accounts affect cash and cash equivalents, and breaks the analysis down to operating, investing, and financing activities.

a. BMC Software, Inc.
c. 3M Company
b. Cash flow statement
d. BNSF Railway

30. According to the Gregorian calendar, the _____ begins on January 1 and ends on December 31.

Generally speaking, a _____ begins on the New Year's Day of the given calendar system and ends on the day before the following New Year's Day. In the Gregorian calendar, this is normally 365 days, but 366 days in a leap year, giving an average length of 365.2425 days.

a. BMC Software, Inc.
c. BNSF Railway
b. 3M Company
d. Calendar year

31. The term _____ refers to government debt, expenditures and revenues, or to finance (particularly financial revenue) in general.

- _____ deficit is the budget deficit of federal or local government
- _____ policy is the discretionary spending of governments. Contrasts with monetary policy.
- _____ year and _____ quarter are reporting periods for firms and other agencies.

See also

- Procurator _____ and Crown Office and Procurator _____ Service

  a. Homogeneous   b. General partner
  c. Fiscal   d. Tertiary sector of economy

32. A _____ is a period used for calculating annual financial statements in businesses and other organizations. In many jurisdictions, regulatory laws regarding accounting and taxation require such reports once per twelve months, but do not require that the period reported on constitutes a calendar year (i.e., January through December.) _____s vary between businesses and countries.

  a. 3M Company   b. Fiscal year
  c. BNSF Railway   d. BMC Software, Inc.

33. _____ is an asset, such as unpaid proceeds from a delivery of goods or services, at which such income item is earned and the related revenue item is recognized, while cash for them is to be received in a latter period, when its amount is deducted from the _____.

  a. Assets   b. Accounts receivable
  c. Accrued expense   d. Accrued revenue

34. In accounting, _____ has a very specific meaning. It is an outflow of cash or other valuable assets from a person or company to another person or company. This outflow of cash is generally one side of a trade for products or services that have equal or better current or future value to the buyer than to the seller.

  a. ABC Television Network   b. AIG
  c. AMEX   d. Expense

35. _____ is equal to the income that a firm has after subtracting costs and expenses from the total revenue. _____ can be distributed among holders of common stock as a dividend or held by the firm as retained earnings.

The items deducted will typically include tax expense, financing expense (interest expense), and minority interest. Likewise, preferred stock dividends will be subtracted too, though they are not an expense.

  a. Long-term liabilities   b. Matching principle
  c. Net income   d. Generally accepted accounting principles

Chapter 5. Accounting for Merchandising Businesses

1. _____ refers to the methods, practices and operations conducted to promote and sustain certain categories of commercial activity. The term is understood to have different specific meanings depending on the context. Merchandise is a sale goods at a store

In marketing, one of the definitions of _____ is the practice in which the brand or image from one product or service is used to sell another.

    a. 3M Company   b. Merchandise
    c. BMC Software, Inc.   d. Merchandising

2. _____ is equal to the income that a firm has after subtracting costs and expenses from the total revenue. _____ can be distributed among holders of common stock as a dividend or held by the firm as retained earnings.

The items deducted will typically include tax expense, financing expense (interest expense), and minority interest. Likewise, preferred stock dividends will be subtracted too, though they are not an expense.

    a. Matching principle   b. Generally accepted accounting principles
    c. Net income   d. Long-term liabilities

3. _____ is a list of the accounts including a unique number of each allowing to locate it in each ledger. The list is typically arranged in the order of the customary appearance of accounts in the financial statements. A _____ can track a specific financial information.

    a. General ledger   b. Journal entry
    c. General journal   d. Chart of accounts

4. In economics, business, retail, and accounting, a _____ is the value of money that has been used up to produce something, and hence is not available for use anymore. In economics, a _____ is an alternative that is given up as a result of a decision. In business, the _____ may be one of acquisition, in which case the amount of money expended to acquire it is counted as _____.

    a. Cost   b. Prime cost
    c. Cost allocation   d. Cost of quality

5. In accounting, _____ or sales profit is the difference between revenue and the cost of making a product or providing a service, before deducting overhead, payroll, taxation, and interest payments. Note that this is different from operating profit (earnings before interest and taxes.)

Net sales are calculated:

        Net sales = Sales - Sales returns and allowances.

    a. Cash flow   b. Public offering
    c. Commercial paper   d. Gross profit

6. Discounting is a financial mechanism in which a debtor obtains the right to delay payments to a creditor, for a defined period of time, in exchange for a charge or fee. Essentially, the party that owes money in the present purchases the right to delay the payment until some future date. The _____, or charge, is simply the difference between the original amount owed in the present and the amount that has to be paid in the future to settle the debt.

a. Risk adjusted return on capital
c. Discount
b. Risk aversion
d. Risk

7. _____ are formal records of a business' financial activities.

In British English, including United Kingdom company law, _____ are often referred to as accounts, although the term _____ is also used, particularly by accountants.

_____ provide an overview of a business' financial condition in both short and long term.

a. 3M Company
c. Financial statements
b. Statement of retained earnings
d. Notes to the financial statements

8. In bookkeeping, accounting, and finance, _____ are operating revenues earned by a company when it sells its products. Revenue (_____) are reported directly on the income statement as Sales or _____.

In financial ratios that use income statement sales values, 'sales' refers to _____, not gross sales.

a. Deferred
c. Historical cost
b. Matching principle
d. Net sales

9. _____ refers to a business or organization attempting to acquire goods or services to accomplish the goals of the enterprise. Though there are several organizations that attempt to set standards in the _____ process, processes can vary greatly between organizations. Typically the word e;_____e; is not used interchangeably with the word e;procuremente;, since procurement typically includes Expediting, Supplier Quality, and Traffic and Logistics (T'L) in addition to _____.

a. Free port
c. Consignor
b. Supply chain
d. Purchasing

10. A _____ is the pinnacle activity involved in selling products or services in return for money or other compensation. It is an act of completion of a commercial activity.

A _____ is completed by the seller, the owner of the goods.

a. Procter ' Gamble
c. Controlled Foreign Corporations
b. Serial bonds
d. Sale

Chapter 5. Accounting for Merchandising Businesses

11. _____ is the process of increasing, or accounting for, an amount over a period of time. Particular instances of the term include:

- _____, the allocation of a lump sum amount to different time periods, particularly for loans and other forms of finance, including related interest or other finance charges.
    - _____ schedule, a table detailing each periodic payment on a loan (typically a mortgage), as generated by an _____ calculator.
    - Negative _____, an _____ schedule where the loan amount actually increases through not paying the full interest
- Amortized analysis, analyzing the execution cost of algorithms over a sequence of operations.
- _____ of capital expenditures of certain assets under accounting rules, particularly intangible assets, in a manner analogous to depreciation.
- _____

   a. Annuity
   c. EBIT
   b. Intangible
   d. Amortization

12. _____ is a company's financial statement that indicates how the revenue is transformed into the net income The purpose of the _____ is to show managers and investors whether the company made or lost money during the period being reported.

The important thing to remember about an _____ is that it represents a period of time.

   a. AIG
   c. Income statement
   b. ABC Television Network
   d. AMEX

13. _____ is a fee paid on borrowed assets. It is the price paid for the use of borrowed money, or, money earned by deposited funds .Assets that are sometimes lent with _____ include money, shares, consumer goods through hire purchase, major assets such as aircraft, and even entire factories in finance lease arrangements. The _____ is calculated upon the value of the assets in the same manner as upon money.

   a. AIG
   c. ABC Television Network
   b. Insolvency
   d. Interest

14. _____ in economics and business is the result of an exchange and from that trade we assign a numerical monetary value to a good, service or asset. If Alice trades Bob 4 apples for an orange, the _____ of an orange is 4 apples. Inversely, the _____ of an apple is 1/4 oranges.

   a. Resale price maintenance
   c. Transactional Net Margin Method
   b. Pricing
   d. Price

15. Transport or _____ is the movement of people and goods from one location to another. Transport is performed by various modes, such as air, rail, road, water, cable, pipeline and space. The field can be divided into infrastructure, vehicles, and operations.

   a. BNSF Railway
   c. 3M Company
   b. BMC Software, Inc.
   d. Transportation

Chapter 5. Accounting for Merchandising Businesses

16. In accounting, _____ has a very specific meaning. It is an outflow of cash or other valuable assets from a person or company to another person or company. This outflow of cash is generally one side of a trade for products or services that have equal or better current or future value to the buyer than to the seller.

   a. AMEX
   b. AIG
   c. ABC Television Network
   d. Expense

17. _____ is the difference between operating revenues and operating expenses, but it is also sometimes used as a synonym for EBIT and operating profit. This is true if the firm has no non-_____.

A professional investor contemplating a change to the capital structure of a firm first evaluates a firm's fundamental earnings potential (reflected by Earnings Before Interest, Taxes, Depreciation and Amortization EBITDA and EBIT), and then determines the optimal use of debt vs. equity.

   a. AMEX
   b. Operating income
   c. ABC Television Network
   d. AIG

18. _____ is a costing model that identifies activities in an organization and assigns the cost of each activity resource to all products and services according to the actual consumption by each: it assigns more indirect costs (overhead) into direct costs.

In this way an organization can establish the true cost of its individual products and services for the purposes of identifying and eliminating those which are unprofitable and lowering the prices of those which are overpriced.

In a business organization, the ABC methodology assigns an organization's resource costs through activities to the products and services provided to its customers.

   a. Activity-based costing
   b. ABC Television Network
   c. Activity-based management
   d. Indirect costs

19. Just in Time could refer to the following:

   - _____, an inventory strategy that reduces in-process inventory
   - _____ compilation, a technique for improving the performance of bytecode-compiled programming systems

   a. Department of the Treasury
   b. Trailing
   c. Price-to-sales ratio
   d. Just-in-time

20. In financial accounting, a _____ or statement of financial position is a summary of a person's or organization's balances. Assets, liabilities and ownership equity are listed as of a specific date, such as the end of its financial year. A _____ is often described as a snapshot of a company's financial condition.

   a. Notes to the financial statements
   b. Statement of retained earnings
   c. Balance sheet
   d. 3M Company

Chapter 5. Accounting for Merchandising Businesses

21. _____ is a specific term used in companies' financial reporting from the company-whole point of view. Because that use excludes the effects of changing ownership interest, an economic measure of _____ is necessary for financial analysis from the shareholders' point of view

_____ is defined by the Financial Accounting Standards Board, or FASB, as 'the change in equity [net assets] of a business enterprise during a period from transactions and other events and circumstances from nonowner sources. It includes all changes in equity during a period except those resulting from investments by owners and distributions to owners.'

_____ is the sum of net income and other items that must bypass the income statement because they have not been realized, including items like an unrealized holding gain or loss from available for sale securities and foreign currency translation gains or losses.

- a. Comprehensive income
- b. BMC Software, Inc.
- c. BNSF Railway
- d. 3M Company

22. The _____, sometimes known as the nominal ledger, is the main accounting record of a business which uses double-entry bookkeeping. It will usually include accounts for such items as current assets, fixed assets, liabilities, revenue and expense items, gains and losses.

The _____ is a collection of the group of accounts that supports the items shown in the major financial statements.

- a. General journal
- b. General ledger
- c. Sales journal
- d. Journal entry

23. _____ is a process by which a firm can obtain the use of a certain fixed assets for which it must pay a series of contractual, periodic, tax deductable payments. The lessee is the receiver of the services or the assets under the lease contract and the lessor is the owner of the assets. The relationship between the tenant and the landlord is called a tenancy, and can be for a fixed or an indefinite period of time (called the term of the lease.)

- a. Due diligence
- b. Tax lien
- c. Limited liability
- d. Leasing

24. A _____, in business matters, is an entity that is controlled by a bigger and more powerful entity. The controlled entity is called a company, corporation, or limited liability company, and the controlling entity is called its parent (or the parent company.) The reason for this distinction is that a lone company cannot be a _____ of any organization; only an entity representing a legal fiction as a separate entity can be a _____.

- a. Subsidiary
- b. Parent company
- c. BMC Software, Inc.
- d. 3M Company

25. _____ is one of a series of accounting transactions dealing with the billing of customers who owe money to a person, company or organization for goods and services that have been provided to the customer. In most business entities this is typically done by generating an invoice and mailing or electronically delivering it to the customer, who in turn must pay it within an established timeframe called credit or payment terms.

Chapter 5. Accounting for Merchandising Businesses

An example of a common payment term is Net 30, meaning payment is due in the amount of the invoice 30 days from the date of invoice.

   a. Adjusting entries
   b. Accrued revenue
   c. Accrual
   d. Accounts receivable

26. In business and accounting, _____ are everything of value that is owned by a person or company. It is a claim on the property your income of a borrower. The balance sheet of a firm records the monetary value of the _____ owned by the firm.
   a. Assets
   b. Accounts receivable
   c. Accrual basis accounting
   d. Earnings before interest, taxes, depreciation and amortization

27. In accounting, the _____ is an account in the general ledger to which a corresponding subsidiary ledger has been created. The subsidiary ledger allows for tracking transactions within the _____ in more detail. Individual transactions are posted both to the _____ and the corresponding subsidiary ledger, and the totals for both are compared when preparing a trial balance to ensure accuracy.
   a. Bookkeeping
   b. Controlling Account
   c. Debit and credit
   d. Debit

28. _____,' also known as property, plant, and equipment (PP&E), is a term used in accountancy for assets and property which cannot easily be converted into cash. This can be compared with current assets such as cash or bank accounts, which are described as liquid assets. In most cases, only tangible assets are referred to as fixed.
   a. Remittance advice
   b. Certified Practising Accountant
   c. Lower of Cost or Market
   d. Fixed asset

29. An _____ or bill is a commercial document issued by a seller to the buyer, indicating the products, quantities, and agreed prices for products or services the seller has provided the buyer. An _____ indicates the buyer must pay the seller, according to the payment terms.

In the rental industry, an _____ must include a specific reference to the duration of the time being billed, so rather than quantity, price and discount the invoicing amount is based on quantity, price, discount and duration.

   a. AMEX
   b. ABC Television Network
   c. Invoice
   d. AIG

30. _____ are formal bookkeeping and accounting terms. They are the most fundamental concepts in accounting, representing the two records that one party in a transaction makes on its records, transferring a money balance from one account to another, one representing a reduction of liability or increase in asset, and the other representing a balancing increase in liability or reduction of asset.

Debits and credits are a system of notation used in accounting to keep track of money movements (transactions) into and out of an account.

Chapter 5. Accounting for Merchandising Businesses

a. Bookkeeping
c. Debit and credit
b. Controlling account
d. Double-entry bookkeeping

31. A _____ is a financial instrument aimed at a reduction in greenhouse gas emissions. _____s are measured in metric tons of carbon dioxide-equivalent (_____$_2$e) and may represent six primary categories of greenhouse gases. One _____ represents the reduction of one metric ton of carbon dioxide or its equivalent in other greenhouse gases.

a. General Accounting Office
c. Sustainable development
b. Carbon offset
d. Mutual fund

32. _____ and credit are formal bookkeeping and accounting terms. They are the most fundamental concepts in accounting, representing the two records that one party in a transaction makes on its records, transferring a money balance from one account to another, one representing a reduction of liability or increase in asset, and the other representing a balancing increase in liability or reduction of asset.

Introduction

_____s and credits are a system of notation used in accounting to keep track of money movements (transactions) into and out of an account.

a. Debit
c. Cookie jar accounting
b. Bookkeeping
d. Double-entry bookkeeping

33. In accounting/accountancy, _____ are journal entries usually made at the end of an accounting period to allocate income and expenditure to the period in which they actually occurred. The revenue recognition principle is the basis of making _____ that pertain to unearned and accrued revenues under accrual-basis accounting. They are sometimes called Balance Day adjustments because they are made on balance day.

a. Adjusting entries
c. Earnings before interest, taxes, depreciation and amortization
b. Accrual
d. Accrued expense

34. In financial accounting the term inventory _____ is the loss of products between point of manufacture or purchase from supplier and point of sale. The term relates to the difference in the amount of margin or profit a retailer can obtain. If the amount of _____ is large, then profits go down which results in increased costs to the consumer to meet the needs of the retailer.

a. Price-to-sales ratio
c. Shrinkage
b. Disclosure
d. Household and Dependent Care Credit

35. _____ are journal entries made at the end of an accounting period to transfer temporary accounts to permanent accounts. An 'income summary' account may be used to show the balance between revenue and expenses, or they could be directly closed against retained earnings where dividend payments will be deducted from. This process is used to reset the balance of these temporary accounts to zero for the next accounting period.

a. Trial balance
c. FIFO and LIFO accounting
b. Treasury stock
d. Closing entries

36. Employment is a contract between two parties, one being the employer and the other being the _____. An _____ may be defined as: 'A person in the service of another under any contract of hire, express or implied, oral or written, where the employer has the power or right to control and direct the _____ in the material details of how the work is to be performed.' Black's Law Dictionary page 471 (5th ed. 1979.)

a. ABC Television Network
b. AIG
c. AMEX
d. Employee

Chapter 6. Inventories

1. _____ also called 'Internal _____'. It is a term of financial audit, internal audit and Enterprise Risk Management. It means the overall attitude, awareness and actions of directors and management (i.e. 'those charged with governance') regarding the internal control system and its importance to the entity.
    a. SOFT audit
    b. Control environment
    c. Trustworthy Repositories Audit ' Certification
    d. Generally accepted auditing standards

2. An _____ or bill is a commercial document issued by a seller to the buyer, indicating the products, quantities, and agreed prices for products or services the seller has provided the buyer. An _____ indicates the buyer must pay the seller, according to the payment terms.

    In the rental industry, an _____ must include a specific reference to the duration of the time being billed, so rather than quantity, price and discount the invoicing amount is based on quantity, price, discount and duration.
    a. ABC Television Network
    b. Invoice
    c. AMEX
    d. AIG

3. A _____ is a commercial document issued by a buyer to a seller, indicating types, quantities, and agreed prices for products or services the seller will provide to the buyer. Sending a _____ to a supplier constitutes a legal offer to buy products or services. Acceptance of a _____ by a seller usually forms a once-off contract between the buyer and seller, so no contract exists until the _____ is accepted.
    a. Voucher
    b. BMC Software, Inc.
    c. Purchase order
    d. 3M Company

4. _____ is a process by which a firm can obtain the use of a certain fixed assets for which it must pay a series of contractual, periodic, tax deductable payments. The lessee is the receiver of the services or the assets under the lease contract and the lessor is the owner of the assets. The relationship between the tenant and the landlord is called a tenancy, and can be for a fixed or an indefinite period of time (called the term of the lease.)
    a. Limited liability
    b. Due diligence
    c. Leasing
    d. Tax lien

5. _____ is a process where a business physically counts its entire inventory. A _____ may be mandated by financial accounting rules or the tax regulations to place an accurate value on the inventory, or the business may need to count inventory so component parts or raw materials can be restocked. Businesses may use several different tactics to minimize the disruption caused by _____.
    a. 3M Company
    b. BMC Software, Inc.
    c. BNSF Railway
    d. Physical inventory

6. In business and accounting, _____ are everything of value that is owned by a person or company. It is a claim on the property your income of a borrower. The balance sheet of a firm records the monetary value of the _____ owned by the firm.
    a. Earnings before interest, taxes, depreciation and amortization
    b. Accounts receivable
    c. Accrual basis accounting
    d. Assets

Chapter 6. Inventories

7. In economics, business, retail, and accounting, a _____ is the value of money that has been used up to produce something, and hence is not available for use anymore. In economics, a _____ is an alternative that is given up as a result of a decision. In business, the _____ may be one of acquisition, in which case the amount of money expended to acquire it is counted as _____.

   a. Cost of quality   b. Cost allocation
   c. Prime cost   d. Cost

8. _____ is the calculated approximation of a result which is usable even if input data may be incomplete or uncertain.

In statistics, see _____ theory, estimator.

In mathematics, approximation or _____ typically means finding upper or lower bounds of a quantity that cannot readily be computed precisely and is also an educated guess .

   a. AMEX   b. Estimation
   c. ABC Television Network   d. AIG

9. _____, also known as property, plant, and equipment (PP&E), is a term used in accountancy for assets and property which cannot easily be converted into cash. This can be compared with current assets such as cash or bank accounts, which are described as liquid assets. In most cases, only tangible assets are referred to as fixed.

   a. Lower of Cost or Market   b. Certified Practising Accountant
   c. Remittance advice   d. Fixed asset

10. Under the average-cost method, it is assumed that the cost of inventory is based on the _____ of the goods available for sale during the period. _____ is computed by dividing the total cost of goods available for sale by the total units available for sale. This gives a weighted-average unit cost that is applied to the units in the ending inventory.

   a. Inventory turnover ratio   b. Average cost
   c. AIG   d. ABC Television Network

11. Under the _____, it is assumed that the cost of inventory is based on the average cost of the goods available for sale during the period. Average cost is computed by dividing the total cost of goods available for sale by the total units available for sale. This gives a weighted-average unit cost that is applied to the units in the ending inventory.

   a. AIG   b. Average-cost method
   c. ABC Television Network   d. AMEX

12. _____ are formal records of a business' financial activities.

In British English, including United Kingdom company law, _____ are often referred to as accounts, although the term _____ is also used, particularly by accountants.

_____ provide an overview of a business' financial condition in both short and long term.

   a. Notes to the financial statements   b. 3M Company
   c. Statement of retained earnings   d. Financial statements

Chapter 6. Inventories

13. A _____ is the transfer of wealth from one party (such as a person or company) to another. A _____ is usually made in exchange for the provision of goods, services or both, or to fulfill a legal obligation.

    The simplest and oldest form of _____ is barter, the exchange of one good or service for another.

    a. 3M Company
    c. Payee
    b. BMC Software, Inc.
    d. Payment

14. In statistics, a _____ is used to analyze a set of data points by creating a series of averages of different subsets of the full data set. So a _____ is not a single number, but it is a set of numbers, each of which is the average of the corresponding subset of a larger set of data points. A simple example is if you had a data set with 100 data points, the first value of the _____ might be the arithmetic mean of data points 1 through 25.

    a. Standard Deviation
    c. Probability distribution
    b. Monte Carlo methods
    d. Moving average

15. In financial accounting, a _____ or statement of financial position is a summary of a person's or organization's balances. Assets, liabilities and ownership equity are listed as of a specific date, such as the end of its financial year. A _____ is often described as a snapshot of a company's financial condition.

    a. Balance sheet
    c. 3M Company
    b. Notes to the financial statements
    d. Statement of retained earnings

16. _____ is an approach to valuing and reporting inventory. Normally ending inventory is stated at historical cost (what was paid to obtain it) but there are times when the original cost of the ending inventory is greater than the cost of replacement thus the inventory has lost value. If the inventory has decreased in value below historical cost then its carrying value is reduced and reported on the balance sheet.

    a. Subledger
    c. Remittance advice
    b. Credit memo
    d. Lower of cost or market

17. In finance, _____ is the process of estimating the potential market value of a financial asset or liability. They can be done on assets (for example, investments in marketable securities such as stocks, options, business enterprises, or intangible assets such as patents and trademarks) or on liabilities (e.g., Bonds issued by a company.) A _____ is required in many contexts including investment analysis, capital budgeting, merger and acquisition transactions, financial reporting, taxable events to determine the proper tax liability, and in litigation.

    a. Daybook
    c. Pay-as-you-go
    b. Capital
    d. Valuation

18. A _____ is any one of a variety of different systems, institutions, procedures, social relations and infrastructures whereby persons trade, and goods and services are exchanged, forming part of the economy. It is an arrangement that allows buyers and sellers to exchange things. _____s vary in size, range, geographic scale, location, types and variety of human communities, as well as the types of goods and services traded.

    a. Market
    c. Recession
    b. Market Failure
    d. Nominal value

Chapter 6. Inventories 43

19. _____ is a method of evaluating an asset's worth when held in inventory, in the field of accounting. _____ is part of the Generally Accepted Accounting Principles that apply to valuing inventory, so as to not overstate or understate the value of inventory goods. Net realisable value is generally equal to the selling price of the inventory goods less the selling costs (completion and disposal).

   a. Net realizable value   b. BMC Software, Inc.
   c. 3M Company   d. Revenue recognition

20. In accounting, the _____ is a worksheet listing the balance at a certain date, of each ledger account in two columns, namely debit and credit. Under the double-entry system, in any transaction the total of any debits must equal the total of any credits, so in a _____ the total of the debit side should always be equal to the total of the credit side. The _____ thus serves as a tool to detect errors, which can result in the totals not being equal.

   a. Depreciation   b. Bottom line
   c. Current asset   d. Trial balance

21. In a contract of carriage, the _____ is the person to whom the shipment is to be delivered whether by land, sea or air.

This is a difficult area of law in that it regulates the mass transportation industry which cannot always guarantee arrival on time or that goods will not be damaged in the course of transit. A further two problems are that unpaid consignors or freight carriers may wish to hold goods until payment is made, and fraudulent individuals may seek to take delivery in place of the legitimate _____s.

   a. Supply chain   b. Purchasing
   c. Consignor   d. Consignee

22. The _____, in a contract of carriage, is the person sending a shipment to be delivered whether by land, sea or air. Some carriers, such as national postal entities, use the term 'sender' or 'shipper' but in the event of a legal dispute the proper and technical term '_____' will generally be used.

If Jones sends a widget to Smith via Fred's Delivery Service, Jones is the _____ and Smith is the consignee.

   a. Consignor   b. Free port
   c. Purchasing   d. Supply chain

23. _____ consists of the sale of goods or merchandise from a fixed location, such as a department store, boutique or kiosk in small or individual lots for direct consumption by the purchaser. _____ may include subordinated services, such as delivery. Purchasers may be individuals or businesses.

   a. BNSF Railway   b. 3M Company
   c. BMC Software, Inc.   d. Retailing

24. In accounting, _____ or sales profit is the difference between revenue and the cost of making a product or providing a service, before deducting overhead, payroll, taxation, and interest payments. Note that this is different from operating profit (earnings before interest and taxes.)

Net sales are calculated:

> Net sales = Sales - Sales returns and allowances.

- a. Gross profit
- b. Commercial paper
- c. Cash flow
- d. Public offering

25. The _____ is an equation that equals the cost of goods sold divided by the average inventory. Average inventory equals beginning inventory plus ending inventory divided by 2.

The formula for _____:

$$\text{Inventory Turnover} = \frac{\text{Cost of Goods Sold}}{\text{Average Inventory}}$$

The formula for average inventory:

$$\text{Average Inventory} = \frac{\text{Beginning inventory} + \text{Ending inventory}}{2}$$

A low turnover rate may point to overstocking, obsolescence, or deficiencies in the product line or marketing effort.

- a. Enterprise Value/Sales
- b. Upside potential ratio
- c. Earnings per share
- d. Inventory turnover

26. _____ is one of a series of accounting transactions dealing with the billing of customers who owe money to a person, company or organization for goods and services that have been provided to the customer. In most business entities this is typically done by generating an invoice and mailing or electronically delivering it to the customer, who in turn must pay it within an established timeframe called credit or payment terms.

An example of a common payment term is Net 30, meaning payment is due in the amount of the invoice 30 days from the date of invoice.

- a. Accounts receivable
- b. Adjusting entries
- c. Accrued revenue
- d. Accrual

27. A _____ is the pinnacle activity involved in selling products or services in return for money or other compensation. It is an act of completion of a commercial activity.

A _____ is completed by the seller, the owner of the goods.

a. Controlled Foreign Corporations
b. Serial bonds
c. Procter ' Gamble
d. Sale

1. _____ also called 'Internal _____'. It is a term of financial audit, internal audit and Enterprise Risk Management. It means the overall attitude, awareness and actions of directors and management (i.e. 'those charged with governance') regarding the internal control system and its importance to the entity.
   a. SOFT audit
   b. Trustworthy Repositories Audit ' Certification
   c. Control environment
   d. Generally accepted auditing standards

2. An _____ is a term used in behavioral economics to describe those types of behaviors that impose costs on a person in the long-run that are not taken into account when making decisions in the present. Classical Economics discourages government from creating legislation that targets internalities, because it is assumed that the consumer takes these personal costs into account when paying for the good that causes the _____. For example, cigarettes should be taxed because of the negative consumption externalities that they impose, such as second-hand smoke, not because the smoker harms him or herself by smoking.
   a. Authorised capital
   b. Inventory turnover ratio
   c. Operating budget
   d. Internality

3. In accounting and organizational theory, _____ is defined as a process effected by an organization's structure, work and authority flows, people and management information systems, designed to help the organization accomplish specific goals or objectives. It is a means by which an organization's resources are directed, monitored, and measured. It plays an important role in preventing and detecting fraud and protecting the organization's resources, both physical (e.g., machinery and property) and intangible (e.g., reputation or intellectual property such as trademarks.)
   a. Audit committee
   b. Audit risk
   c. Auditor independence
   d. Internal Control

4. The _____ of 2002 (Pub.L. 107-204, 116 Stat. 745, enacted July 30, 2002), also known as the Public Company Accounting Reform and Investor Protection Act of 2002, is a United States federal law enacted on July 30, 2002 in response to a number of major corporate and accounting scandals including those affecting Enron, Tyco International, Adelphia, Peregrine Systems and WorldCom. The legislation establishes new or enhanced standards for all U.S. public company boards, management, and public accounting firms. It does not apply to privately held companies.
   a. Sarbanes-Oxley Act
   b. Staple right
   c. Burden of proof
   d. Tax lien

5. Employment is a contract between two parties, one being the employer and the other being the _____. An _____ may be defined as: 'A person in the service of another under any contract of hire, express or implied, oral or written, where the employer has the power or right to control and direct the _____ in the material details of how the work is to be performed.' Black's Law Dictionary page 471 (5th ed. 1979.)
   a. AIG
   b. ABC Television Network
   c. AMEX
   d. Employee

6. Established in 1988 the _____ is the professional organization that governs professional fraud examiners. Its activities include producing fraud information, tools and training. It also governs the professional designation of Certified Fraud Examiner.
   a. Association of Certified Fraud Examiners
   b. ABC Television Network
   c. AIG
   d. AMEX

7. _____ is a designation awarded by the Association of _____s (ACertified Fraud Examiner.) The ACertified Fraud Examiner is a 41,000 member-based global association dedicated to providing anti-fraud education and training.

In order to become a _____ one must meet the following requirements:

- Be an Associate Member of the ACertified Fraud Examiner in good standing
- Meet minimum academic and professional requirements
- Be of high moral character
- Agree to abide by the Bylaws and Code of Professional Ethics of the Association of _____s

Generally, applicants for _____ certification have a minimum of a bachelor's degree or equivalent from an institution of higher education. Two years of professional experience related to fraud can be substituted for each year of college.

a. Certified General Accountant
b. Certified public accountant
c. Chartered Accountant
d. Certified Fraud Examiner

8. An _____ is a mostly hierarchical concept of subordination of entities that collaborate and contribute to serve one common aim.

Organizations are a variant of clustered entities. The structure of an organization is usually set up in many a styles, dependent on their objectives and ambience.

a. AIG
b. AMEX
c. ABC Television Network
d. Organizational structure

9. _____ is a concept that denotes the precise probability of specific eventualities. Technically, the notion of _____ is independent from the notion of value and, as such, eventualities may have both beneficial and adverse consequences. However, in general usage the convention is to focus only on potential negative impact to some characteristic of value that may arise from a future event.

a. Discount
b. Risk adjusted return on capital
c. Discounting
d. Risk

10. _____ is a step in a risk management process. _____ is the determination of quantitative or qualitative value of risk related to a concrete situation and a recognized threat (also called hazard.) Quantitative _____ requires calculations of two components of risk: R, the magnitude of the potential loss L, and the probability p that the loss will occur.

a. BMC Software, Inc.
b. BNSF Railway
c. 3M Company
d. Risk assessment

11. In business and accounting, _____ are everything of value that is owned by a person or company. It is a claim on the property your income of a borrower. The balance sheet of a firm records the monetary value of the _____ owned by the firm.

a. Earnings before interest, taxes, depreciation and amortization
b. Accounts receivable
c. Accrual basis accounting
d. Assets

Chapter 7. Sarbanes-Oxley, Internal Control, and Cash

12. Just in Time could refer to the following:

   - _____, an inventory strategy that reduces in-process inventory
   - _____ compilation, a technique for improving the performance of bytecode-compiled programming systems

   a. Trailing
   b. Department of the Treasury
   c. Just-in-time
   d. Price-to-sales ratio

13. In physics, and more specifically kinematics, _____ is the change in velocity over time. Because velocity is a vector, it can change in two ways: a change in magnitude and/or a change in direction. In one dimension, _____ is the rate at which something speeds up or slows down.

   a. AMEX
   b. AIG
   c. Acceleration
   d. ABC Television Network

14. The _____ is the current method of accelerated asset depreciation required by the United States income tax code. Under _____, all assets are divided into classes which dictate the number of years over which an asset's cost will be recovered.

   Prior to the Accelerated Cost Recovery System (ACRS), most capital purchases were depreciated using a straight line technique, that allowed for the depreciation of the asset over its useful life.

   a. Modified Accelerated Cost Recovery System
   b. Categorical grants
   c. BMC Software, Inc.
   d. 3M Company

15. In economics, business, retail, and accounting, a _____ is the value of money that has been used up to produce something, and hence is not available for use anymore. In economics, a _____ is an alternative that is given up as a result of a decision. In business, the _____ may be one of acquisition, in which case the amount of money expended to acquire it is counted as _____.

   a. Cost
   b. Prime cost
   c. Cost allocation
   d. Cost of quality

16. The _____ is a private, not-for-profit organization whose primary purpose is to develop generally accepted accounting principles (GAAP) within the United States in the public's interest. The Securities and Exchange Commission (SEC) designated the _____ as the organization responsible for setting accounting standards for public companies in the U.S. It was created in 1973, replacing the Accounting Principles Board and the Committee on Accounting Procedure of the American Institute of Certified Public Accountants. The _____'s mission is 'to establish and improve standards of financial accounting and reporting for the guidance and education of the public, including issuers, auditors, and users of financial information.'

   The _____ is not a governmental body.

   a. Privately held
   b. Public company
   c. Governmental Accounting Standards Board
   d. Financial Accounting Standards Board

Chapter 7. Sarbanes-Oxley, Internal Control, and Cash

17. A _____ is a fungible, negotiable instrument representing financial value. they are broadly categorized into debt securities (such as banknotes, bonds and debentures), and equity securities; e.g., common stocks. The company or other entity issuing the _____ is called the issuer.

   a. Tracking stock
                                       b. BMC Software, Inc.
   c. 3M Company
                                       d. Security

18. A _____ is the transfer of wealth from one party (such as a person or company) to another. A _____ is usually made in exchange for the provision of goods, services or both, or to fulfill a legal obligation.

The simplest and oldest form of _____ is barter, the exchange of one good or service for another.

   a. 3M Company
                                        b. Payee
   c. BMC Software, Inc.
                                d. Payment

19. A _____ is the pinnacle activity involved in selling products or services in return for money or other compensation. It is an act of completion of a commercial activity.

A _____ is completed by the seller, the owner of the goods.

   a. Serial bonds
                                      b. Controlled Foreign Corporations
   c. Sale
                                        d. Procter ' Gamble

20. _____ refers to the computer-based systems used to perform financial transactions electronically.

The term is used for a number of different concepts:

- Cardholder-initiated transactions, where a cardholder makes use of a payment card
- Direct deposit payroll payments for a business to its employees, possibly via a payroll services company
- Direct debit payments from customer to business, where the transaction is initiated by the business with customer permission
- Electronic bill payment in online banking, which may be delivered by _____ or paper check
- Transactions involving stored value of electronic money, possibly in a private currency
- Wire transfer via an international banking network (generally carries a higher fee)
- Electronic Benefit Transfer

electronic funds transferPOS (short for _____ at Point of Sale) is an Australian and New Zealand electronic processing system for credit cards, debit cards and charge cards.

European banks and card companies also sometimes reference 'electronic funds transferPOS' as the system used for processing card transactions through terminals on points of sale, though the system is not the trademarked Australian/New Zealand variant.

Credit cards

_____ may be initiated by a cardholder when a payment card such as a credit card or debit card is used.

a. AIG
b. AMEX
c. Electronic funds transfer
d. ABC Television Network

21. A _____ is a letter sent by a customer to a supplier, to inform the supplier that his invoice has been paid. If the customer is paying by cheque, the _____ often accompanies the cheque.

_____s are not mandatory, but they are seen as a courtesy, because they help the supplier's accounts department to match invoices with payments.

a. Subledger
b. Lower of Cost or Market
c. Certified Practising Accountant
d. Remittance advice

22. A _____ is a bond which is worth a certain monetary value and which may only be spent for specific reasons or on specific goods. Examples include -- but are not limited to -- housing, travel and food _____s. The term _____ is also a synonym for receipt, and is often used to refer to receipts used as evidence of, for example, the declaration that a service has been performed or that an expenditure has been made.

a. BMC Software, Inc.
b. 3M Company
c. Source document
d. Voucher

23. An account statement or a _____ is a summary of all financial transactions occurring over a given period of time on a deposit account, a credit card, or any other type of account offered by a financial institution.

_____s are typically printed on one or several pieces of paper and either mailed directly to the account holder's address, or kept at the financial institution's local branch for pick-up. Certain ATMs offer the possibility to print, at any time, a condensed version of a _____.

a. BNSF Railway
b. 3M Company
c. Bank statement
d. BMC Software, Inc.

24. _____ refers to a category of criminal acts that involve making the unlawful use of checks in order to illegally acquire or borrow funds that do not exist within the account balance or account-holder's legal ownership. Most methods involve taking advantage of the float (the time between the negotiation of the cheque and its clearance at the cheque-writer's bank) to draw out these funds. Specific kinds of cheque fraud include cheque kiting, where funds are deposited before the end of the float period to cover the fraud, and paper hanging, where the float offers the opportunity to commit the crime but the account is never replenished.

a. 3M Company
b. BMC Software, Inc.
c. BNSF Railway
d. Check fraud

25. _____ is the process of matching and comparing figures from accounting records against those presented on a bank statement. Less any items which have no relation to the bank statement, the balance of the accounting ledger should reconcile (match) to the balance of the bank statement.

_____ allows companies or individuals to compare their account records to the bank's records of their account balance in order to uncover any possible discrepancies.

a. Remittance advice
c. Bankruptcy prediction
b. Bank reconciliation
d. Certified Practising Accountant

26. _____ is often a small amount of discretionary funds in the form of cash used for expenditures where it is not sensible to make the disbursement by check, because of the inconvenience and costs of writing, signing and then cashing the check.

The most common way of accounting expenditures is to use the imprest system. The initial fund would be created by issuing a check for the desired amount.

a. Petty cash
c. Fixed asset
b. Remittance advice
d. Minority interest

27. _____ are the most liquid assets found within the asset portion of a company's balance sheet. Cash equivalents are assets that are readily convertible into cash, such as money market holdings, short-term government bonds or Treasury bills, marketable securities and commercial paper. _____ are distinguished from other investments through their short-term existence; they mature within 3 months whereas short-term investments are 12 months or less, and long-term investments are any investments that mature in excess of 12 months.

a. Money market
c. Creditor
b. Restructuring
d. Cash and cash equivalents

28. A _____ is any credit facility extended to a business by a bank or financial institution. A _____ may take several forms such as cash credit, overdraft, demand loan, export packing credit, term loan, discounting or purchase of commercial bills etc. It is like an account that can readily be tapped into if the need arises or not touched at all and saved for emergencies.

a. Simple interest
c. 3M Company
b. BMC Software, Inc.
d. Line of credit

Chapter 8. Receivables

1. _____ is one of a series of accounting transactions dealing with the billing of customers who owe money to a person, company or organization for goods and services that have been provided to the customer. In most business entities this is typically done by generating an invoice and mailing or electronically delivering it to the customer, who in turn must pay it within an established timeframe called credit or payment terms.

An example of a common payment term is Net 30, meaning payment is due in the amount of the invoice 30 days from the date of invoice.

   a. Accounts receivable
   b. Accrued revenue
   c. Adjusting entries
   d. Accrual

2. _____ represents claims for which formal instruments of credit are issued as evidence of debt, such as a promissory note. The credit instrument normally requires the debtor to pay interest and extends for time periods of 60-90 days or longer.
   a. Notes receivable
   b. Restricted stock
   c. Moving average
   d. Public offering

3. A _____, in business matters, is an entity that is controlled by a bigger and more powerful entity. The controlled entity is called a company, corporation, or limited liability company, and the controlling entity is called its parent (or the parent company.) The reason for this distinction is that a lone company cannot be a _____ of any organization; only an entity representing a legal fiction as a separate entity can be a _____.
   a. Parent company
   b. 3M Company
   c. BMC Software, Inc.
   d. Subsidiary

4. The _____ is a subset of the general ledger used in accounting. The _____ shows detail for part of the accounting records such as property and equipment, prepaid expenses, etc. The detail would include such items as date the item was purchased or expense incurred, a description of the item, the original balance, and the net book value.
   a. Credit memo
   b. Remittance advice
   c. Minority interest
   d. Subledger

5. In financial accounting and finance, _____ is the portion of receivables that can no longer be collected, typically from accounts receivable or loans. _____ in accounting is considered an expense.

There are two methods to account for _____:

   1. Direct write off method (Non - GAAP)

A receivable which is not considered collectible is charged directly to the income statement.

   1. Allowance method (GAAP)

An estimate is made at the end of each fiscal year of the amount of _____. This is then accumulated in a provision which is then used to reduce specific receivable accounts as and when necessary.

   a. Total Expense Ratio
   b. 3M Company
   c. Payroll
   d. Bad debt

Chapter 8. Receivables

6. In accounting, _____ has a very specific meaning. It is an outflow of cash or other valuable assets from a person or company to another person or company. This outflow of cash is generally one side of a trade for products or services that have equal or better current or future value to the buyer than to the seller.

   a. AMEX
   b. AIG
   c. ABC Television Network
   d. Expense

7. In mathematics _____s are numbers or other things that get multiplied. In particular, see:

   - Factorization, the decomposition of an object into a product of other objects
   - Integer factorization, the process of breaking down a composite number into smaller non-trivial divisors
   - A coefficient
   - A divisor of a particular number, or of an element of a monoid
   - A von Neumann algebra with a trivial center

   In statistics

   - _____ analysis is the study of how _____s or certain variables affect variables.

   In technology:

   - Human _____s, a profession that focuses on how people interact with products, tools, or procedures
   - 'Functionality, Application domain, Conditions, Technology, Objects and Responsibility;', In object-oriented programming

   In computer science and information technology:

   - Authentication _____, a piece of information used to verify a person's identity for security purposes
   - _____, a Unix command for numbers factorization
   - _____ (programming language), an experimental Forth-like programming language

   In television:

   - The O'Reilly _____, an American talk show hosted by Bill O'Reilly on Fox News.
   - The Krypton _____, a British game show hosted by Gordon Burns, formally on ITV. Also had an American version.

   .
   a. Factor
   b. Markup
   c. Household and Dependent Care Credit
   d. Sale

8. _____ is that which is owed; usually referencing assets owed, but the term can also cover moral obligations and other interactions not requiring money. In the case of assets, _____ is a means of using future purchasing power in the present before a summation has been earned. Some companies and corporations use _____ as a part of their overall corporate finance strategy.

a. Lender
b. Debenture
c. Loan
d. Debt

9. The term _____ describes a reduction in recognized value. In accounting terminology, it refers to recognition of the reduced or zero value of an asset. In income tax statements, it refers to a reduction of taxable income as recognition of certain expenses required to produce the income.
  a. Write-off
  b. Current asset
  c. Salvage value
  d. Payroll

10. The term _____ or superannuation refers to a pension granted upon retirement. They may be set up by employers, insurance companies, the government or other institutions such as employer associations or trade unions.
  a. 3M Company
  b. BMC Software, Inc.
  c. Retirement plan
  d. Wage

11. _____ is a method of evaluating an asset's worth when held in inventory, in the field of accounting. _____ is part of the Generally Accepted Accounting Principles that apply to valuing inventory, so as to not overstate or understate the value of inventory goods. Net realisable value is generally equal to the selling price of the inventory goods less the selling costs (completion and disposal).
  a. 3M Company
  b. Revenue recognition
  c. BMC Software, Inc.
  d. Net realizable value

12. _____ is the calculated approximation of a result which is usable even if input data may be incomplete or uncertain.

In statistics, see _____ theory, estimator.

In mathematics, approximation or _____ typically means finding upper or lower bounds of a quantity that cannot readily be computed precisely and is also an educated guess .

  a. Estimation
  b. AIG
  c. ABC Television Network
  d. AMEX

13. A _____ is the pinnacle activity involved in selling products or services in return for money or other compensation. It is an act of completion of a commercial activity.

A _____ is completed by the seller, the owner of the goods.

  a. Controlled Foreign Corporations
  b. Serial bonds
  c. Procter ' Gamble
  d. Sale

14. A _____ is the date when a given thing is expected to arrive (when it is due which has a meaning similar to 'owe'.)

In homework, the _____ is the date by which the homework must be handed in. Similarly, many other assignments in the business and public worlds have dates by which the task must be completed and returned to the person who assigned the task, their _____s.

Chapter 8. Receivables

a. Due date
b. BNSF Railway
c. 3M Company
d. BMC Software, Inc.

15. _____ is a life of security. It may also refer to the final payment date of a loan or other financial instrument, at which point all remaining interest and principal is due to be paid.

1, 3, 6 months _____ band can be calculated by using 30-day per month periods. For _____ bands over a year it is acceptable to use 365 day per year. For example with a Treasury Bond, its _____ is the date on which the principal is paid.

a. Screening
b. Maturity
c. Serial bonds
d. Markup

16. In law, the payer is the party making a payment while the _____ is the party receiving the payment.

There are two types of payment methods; exchanging and provisioning. Exchanging is to change coin, money and banknote in terms of the price.

a. Payment
b. BMC Software, Inc.
c. Payee
d. 3M Company

17. In finance, a _____ is a debt security, in which the authorized issuer owes the holders a debt and, depending on the terms of the _____, is obliged to pay interest (the coupon) and/or to repay the principal at a later date, termed maturity. It is a formal contract to repay borrowed money with interest at fixed intervals.

Thus a _____ is like a loan: the issuer is the borrower, the _____ holder is the lender, and the coupon is the interest.

a. Revenue bonds
b. Zero-coupon bond
c. Bond
d. Coupon rate

18. In financial accounting, a _____ or statement of financial position is a summary of a person's or organization's balances. Assets, liabilities and ownership equity are listed as of a specific date, such as the end of its financial year. A _____ is often described as a snapshot of a company's financial condition.

a. Statement of retained earnings
b. Notes to the financial statements
c. 3M Company
d. Balance sheet

19. _____ that may or may not be incurred by an entity depending on the outcome of a future event such as a court case. These liabilities are recorded in a company's accounts and shown in the balance sheet when both probable and reasonably estimable. A footnote to the balance sheet describes the nature and extent of the _____.

a. Headnote
b. Nonacquiescence
c. Tangible
d. Contingent liabilities

20. _____ is a financial mechanism in which a debtor obtains the right to delay payments to a creditor, for a defined period of time, in exchange for a charge or fee. Essentially, the party that owes money in the present purchases the right to delay the payment until some future date. The discount, or charge, is simply the difference between the original amount owed in the present and the amount that has to be paid in the future to settle the debt.
- a. Risk adjusted return on capital
- b. Risk aversion
- c. Discount factor
- d. Discounting

21. In financial accounting, a _____ is defined as an obligation of an entity arising from past transactions or events, the settlement of which may result in the transfer or use of assets, provision of services or other yielding of economic benefits in the future.
- a. Resource Conservation and Recovery Act
- b. Liability
- c. Pre-emption right
- d. Trust Indenture Act of 1939

Chapter 9. Fixed Assets and Intangible Assets

1. In business and accounting, _____ are everything of value that is owned by a person or company. It is a claim on the property your income of a borrower. The balance sheet of a firm records the monetary value of the _____ owned by the firm.

   a. Assets
   b. Earnings before interest, taxes, depreciation and amortization
   c. Accrual basis accounting
   d. Accounts receivable

2. In economics, business, retail, and accounting, a _____ is the value of money that has been used up to produce something, and hence is not available for use anymore. In economics, a _____ is an alternative that is given up as a result of a decision. In business, the _____ may be one of acquisition, in which case the amount of money expended to acquire it is counted as _____.

   a. Cost of quality
   b. Cost allocation
   c. Cost
   d. Prime cost

3. _____, also known as property, plant, and equipment (PP&E), is a term used in accountancy for assets and property which cannot easily be converted into cash. This can be compared with current assets such as cash or bank accounts, which are described as liquid assets. In most cases, only tangible assets are referred to as fixed.

   a. Lower of Cost or Market
   b. Remittance advice
   c. Certified Practising Accountant
   d. Fixed asset

4. _____ is any physical or virtual entity that is owned by an individual or jointly by a group of individuals. An owner of _____ has the right to consume, sell, rent, mortgage, transfer and exchange his or her _____. Important widely-recognized types of _____ include real _____, personal _____ (other physical possessions), and intellectual _____ (rights over artistic creations, inventions, etc.), although the latter is not always as widely recognized or enforced.

   a. Corporate governance
   b. Board of directors
   c. Limited liability
   d. Property

5. In law, tangibility is the attribute of being detectable with the senses.

   In criminal law, one of the elements of an offense of larceny is that the stolen property must be _____.

   In the context of intellectual property, expression in _____ form is one of the requirements for copyright protection.

   a. Nonacquiescence
   b. Headnote
   c. Contingent liabilities
   d. Tangible

6. In economics, _____ or _____ goods or real _____ refers to factors of production used to create goods or services that are not themselves significantly consumed (though they may depreciate) in the production process. _____ goods may be acquired with money or financial _____. In finance and accounting, _____ generally refers to financial wealth, especially that used to start or maintain a business.

   a. Consumption
   b. Sale
   c. Capital
   d. Debt-to-GDP ratios

Chapter 9. Fixed Assets and Intangible Assets

7. A _____ is an expenditure creating future benefits. A _____ is incurred when a business spends money either to buy fixed assets or to add to the value of an existing fixed asset with a useful life that extends beyond the taxable year. Capex are used by a company to acquire or upgrade physical assets such as equipment, property, or industrial buildings.
   a. BMC Software, Inc.
   b. 3M Company
   c. Capital flight
   d. Capital expenditure

8. An _____, operating expenditure, operational expense, operational expenditure or OPEX is an on-going cost for running a product, business, or system. Its counterpart, a capital expenditure (CAPEX), is the cost of developing or providing non-consumable parts for the product or system. For example, the purchase of a photocopier is the CAPEX, and the annual paper and toner cost is the OPEX.
   a. AIG
   b. Operating expense
   c. AMEX
   d. ABC Television Network

9. _____ is fixing any sort of mechanical or electrical device should it become out of order or broken (known as repair or unscheduled maintenance) as well as performing the routine actions which keep the device in working order (known as scheduled maintenance) or prevent trouble from arising (preventive maintenance.) The MRO business is seeing a major boom with the emergence of international carriers and private aviation in Asia. The MRO business in India alone is expected to grow to $45Bn from the current $0.5Bn in the next decade.
   a. 3M Company
   b. BNSF Railway
   c. Maintenance, repair and operations
   d. BMC Software, Inc.

10. _____ is a type of lease - the other being an operating lease. A _____ effectively allows a firm to finance the purchase of an asset, even if, strictly speaking, the firm never acquires the asset. Typically, a _____ will give the lessee control over an asset for a large proportion of the asset's useful life, providing them the benefits and risks of ownership.
    a. 3M Company
    b. Finance lease
    c. Debt ratio
    d. Profitability index

11. A _____ is a contract conferring a right on one person to possess property belonging to another person (called a landlord or lessor) to the exclusion of the owner landlord. It is a rental agreement between landlord and tenant. The relationship between the tenant and the landlord is called a tenancy, and the right to possession by the tenant is sometimes called a leasehold interest.
    a. Lease
    b. Fraud Enforcement and Recovery Act
    c. Board of directors
    d. Types of business

12. _____ is a process by which a firm can obtain the use of a certain fixed assets for which it must pay a series of contractual, periodic, tax deductable payments. The lessee is the receiver of the services or the assets under the lease contract and the lessor is the owner of the assets. The relationship between the tenant and the landlord is called a tenancy, and can be for a fixed or an indefinite period of time (called the term of the lease.)
    a. Limited liability
    b. Leasing
    c. Due diligence
    d. Tax lien

13. An _____ is a lease whose term is short compared to the useful life of the asset or piece of equipment (an airliner, a ship etc.) being leased. An _____ is commonly used to acquire equipment on a relatively short-term basis.

Chapter 9. Fixed Assets and Intangible Assets

a. Operating lease
c. Express warranty
b. Employee Retirement Income Security Act
d. Issued shares

14. _____ is a term used in accounting, economics and finance to spread the cost of an asset over the span of several years.

In simple words we can say that _____ is the reduction in the value of an asset due to usage, passage of time, wear and tear, technological outdating or obsolescence, depletion, inadequacy, rot, rust, decay or other such factors.

In accounting, _____ is a term used to describe any method of attributing the historical or purchase cost of an asset across its useful life, roughly corresponding to normal wear and tear.

a. Net profit
c. Current asset
b. General ledger
d. Depreciation

15. In accounting, _____ has a very specific meaning. It is an outflow of cash or other valuable assets from a person or company to another person or company. This outflow of cash is generally one side of a trade for products or services that have equal or better current or future value to the buyer than to the seller.
a. Expense
c. AIG
b. ABC Television Network
d. AMEX

16. In mathematics _____s are numbers or other things that get multiplied. In particular, see:

- Factorization, the decomposition of an object into a product of other objects
- Integer factorization, the process of breaking down a composite number into smaller non-trivial divisors
- A coefficient
- A divisor of a particular number, or of an element of a monoid
- A von Neumann algebra with a trivial center

In statistics

- _____ analysis is the study of how _____s or certain variables affect variables.

In technology:

- Human _____s, a profession that focuses on how people interact with products, tools, or procedures
- 'Functionality, Application domain, Conditions, Technology, Objects and Responsibility;', In object-oriented programming

Chapter 9. Fixed Assets and Intangible Assets

In computer science and information technology:

- Authentication _____, a piece of information used to verify a person's identity for security purposes
- _____, a Unix command for numbers factorization
- _____ (programming language), an experimental Forth-like programming language

In television:

- The O'Reilly _____, an American talk show hosted by Bill O'Reilly on Fox News.
- The Krypton _____, a British game show hosted by Gordon Burns, formally on ITV. Also had an American version.

a. Factor
b. Markup
c. Household and Dependent Care Credit
d. Sale

17. The _____ is the current method of accelerated asset depreciation required by the United States income tax code. Under _____, all assets are divided into classes which dictate the number of years over which an asset's cost will be recovered.

Prior to the Accelerated Cost Recovery System (ACRS), most capital purchases were depreciated using a straight line technique, that allowed for the depreciation of the asset over its useful life.

a. 3M Company
b. Categorical grants
c. BMC Software, Inc.
d. Modified Accelerated Cost Recovery System

18. _____ is one of the constituents of a leasing calculus or operation. It describes the future value of a good in terms of percentage of depreciation of its initial value.

a. 3M Company
b. Residual value
c. Net pay
d. Round-tripping

19. Straight-line depreciation is the simplest and most often used technique, in which the company estimates the _____ of the asset at the end of the period during which it will be used to generate revenues (useful life), and will expense a portion of original cost in equal increments over that period. The _____ is an estimate of the value of the asset at the time it will be sold or disposed of; it may be zero. _____ is scrap value, by another name.

a. Closing entries
b. Salvage value
c. Net profit
d. Generally accepted accounting principles

20. Book Value = Original Cost - _____

Book value at the end of year becomes book value at the beginning of next year. The asset is depreciated until the book value equals scrap value.

Chapter 9. Fixed Assets and Intangible Assets   61

If the vehicle were to be sold and the sales price exceeded the depreciated value (net book value) then the excess would be considered a gain and subject to depreciation recapture.

    a. AIG
    b. ABC Television Network
    c. AMEX
    d. Accumulated Depreciation

21. In finance, a _____ is a debt security, in which the authorized issuer owes the holders a debt and, depending on the terms of the _____, is obliged to pay interest (the coupon) and/or to repay the principal at a later date, termed maturity. It is a formal contract to repay borrowed money with interest at fixed intervals.

Thus a _____ is like a loan: the issuer is the borrower, the _____ holder is the lender, and the coupon is the interest.

    a. Revenue bonds
    b. Coupon rate
    c. Zero-coupon bond
    d. Bond

22. There are several methods for calculating depreciation, generally based on either the passage of time or the level of activity (or use) of the asset.

_____ is the simplest and most often used technique, in which the company estimates the salvage value of the asset at the end of the period during which it will be used to generate revenues (useful life), and will expense a portion of original cost in equal increments over that period.

    a. Current asset
    b. Pro forma
    c. Closing entries
    d. Straight-line depreciation

23. In accounting, _____ or carrying value is the value of an asset according to its balance sheet account balance. For assets, the value is based on the original cost of the asset less any depreciation, amortization or impairment costs made against the asset. Traditionally, a company's _____ is its total assets minus intangible assets and liabilities.

    a. Book value
    b. Generally accepted accounting principles
    c. Matching principle
    d. Depreciation

24. In physics, and more specifically kinematics, _____ is the change in velocity over time. Because velocity is a vector, it can change in two ways: a change in magnitude and/or a change in direction. In one dimension, _____ is the rate at which something speeds up or slows down.

    a. AMEX
    b. ABC Television Network
    c. Acceleration
    d. AIG

25. _____ refers to any one of several methods by which a company, for 'financial accounting' and/or tax purposes, depreciates a fixed asset in such a way that the amount of depreciation taken each year is higher during the earlier years of an assete;s life. For financial accounting purposes, _____ is generally used when an asset is expected to be much more productive during its early years, so that depreciation expense will more accurately represent how much of an assete;s usefulness is being used up each year. For tax purposes, _____ provides a way of deferring corporate income taxes by reducing taxable income in current years, in exchange for increased taxable income in future years.

Chapter 9. Fixed Assets and Intangible Assets

a. Accelerated depreciation
b. Indirect tax
c. Effective marginal tax rates
d. User charge

26. An _____ is a tax levied on the financial income of people, corporations, or other legal entities. Various _____ systems exist, with varying degrees of tax incidence. Income taxation can be progressive, proportional, or regressive.
   a. Individual Retirement Arrangement
   b. Ordinary income
   c. Implied level of government service
   d. Income tax

27. An _____ is a term used in behavioral economics to describe those types of behaviors that impose costs on a person in the long-run that are not taken into account when making decisions in the present. Classical Economics discourages government from creating legislation that targets internalities, because it is assumed that the consumer takes these personal costs into account when paying for the good that causes the _____. For example, cigarettes should be taxed because of the negative consumption externalities that they impose, such as second-hand smoke, not because the smoker harms him or herself by smoking.
   a. Operating budget
   b. Inventory turnover ratio
   c. Authorised capital
   d. Internality

28. The _____ is the main body of domestic statutory tax law of the United States organized topically, including laws covering the income tax , payroll taxes, gift taxes, estate taxes and statutory excise taxes. The _____ is published as Title 26 of the United States Code (USC), and is also known as the internal revenue title.
   a. Income tax
   b. Ordinary income
   c. Equity of condition
   d. Internal Revenue Code

29. _____ is the process of increasing, or accounting for, an amount over a period of time. Particular instances of the term include:

   - _____, the allocation of a lump sum amount to different time periods, particularly for loans and other forms of finance, including related interest or other finance charges.
     - _____ schedule, a table detailing each periodic payment on a loan (typically a mortgage), as generated by an _____ calculator.
     - Negative _____, an _____ schedule where the loan amount actually increases through not paying the full interest
   - Amortized analysis, analyzing the execution cost of algorithms over a sequence of operations.
   - _____ of capital expenditures of certain assets under accounting rules, particularly intangible assets, in a manner analogous to depreciation.
   - _____

   a. Amortization
   b. EBIT
   c. Intangible
   d. Annuity

30. A _____ is a set of exclusive rights granted by a state to an inventor or his assignee for a limited period of time in exchange for a disclosure of an invention.

Chapter 9. Fixed Assets and Intangible Assets

The procedure for granting _____s, the requirements placed on the _____ee and the extent of the exclusive rights vary widely between countries according to national laws and international agreements. Typically, however, a _____ application must include one or more claims defining the invention which must be new, inventive, and useful or industrially applicable.

    a. National Information Infrastructure Protection Act   b. Foreign Corrupt Practices Act
    c. Model Code of Professional Responsibility   d. Patent

31. The phrase _____, according to the Organization for Economic Co-operation and Development, refers to 'creative work undertaken on a systematic basis in order to increase the stock of knowledge, including knowledge of man, culture and society, and the use of this stock of knowledge to devise new applications [sic]'

New product design and development is more than often a crucial factor in the survival of a company. In an industry that is fast changing, firms must continually revise their design and range of products. This is necessary due to continuous technology change and development as well as other competitors and the changing preference of customers.

    a. 3M Company   b. BNSF Railway
    c. BMC Software, Inc.   d. Research and development

32. _____ are defined as identifiable non-monetary assets that cannot be seen, touched or physically measured, which are created through time and/or effort and that are identifiable as a separate asset. There are two primary forms of intangibles - legal intangibles (such as trade secrets (e.g., customer lists), copyrights, patents, trademarks, and goodwill) and competitive intangibles (such as knowledge activities (know-how, knowledge), collaboration activities, leverage activities, and structural activities.) Legal intangibles are known under the generic term intellectual property and generate legal property rights defensible in a court of law.

    a. ABC Television Network   b. Intangible assets
    c. AIG   d. Overhead

33. A _____ or trade mark, identified by the symbols ™ (not yet registered) and ® (registered), is a distinctive sign or indicator used by an individual, business organization or other legal entity to identify that the products and/or services to consumers with which the _____ appears originate from a unique source, and to distinguish its products or services from those of other entities. A _____ is a type of intellectual property, and typically a name, word, phrase, logo, symbol, design, image, or a combination of these elements. There is also a range of non-conventional _____s comprising marks which do not fall into these standard categories.

    a. Kanban   b. Trademark
    c. FIFO   d. Risk management

Chapter 9. Fixed Assets and Intangible Assets

34. _____ means the giving out of information, either voluntarily or to be in compliance with legal regulations or workplace rules.

- In Computer security, full _____ means disclosing full information about vulnerabilities.
- In computing, _____ widget
- Journalism, full _____ refers to disclosing the interests of the writer which may bear on the subject being written about, for example, if the writer has worked with an interview subject in the past.

- In law:
    - The law of England and Wales, _____ refers to a process that may form part of legal proceedings, whereby parties inform to other parties the existence of any relevant documents that are, or have been, in their control. This compares with the process known as discovery in the course of legal proceedings in the United States.
    - In U.S. civil procedure (litigation rules for civil cases), _____ is a stage prior to trial. In civil cases, each party must disclose to the opposing party the following: names of witnesses which it may use to support its side, copies of documents (or mere description of these documents) in its control which it may use to support its side, computation of damages claimed, and certain insurance information. _____ is related to, but technically prior to, the discovery stage.
    - In Company law (known as 'corporate law' in the United States), _____ refers to giving out information about public or limited companies or their officers, which might be kept secret if the company was a private company or a partnership.

- In real property transactions, _____ refers to providing to a buyer information known to the seller or broker/agent concerning the condition or other aspects of real property that would affect the property's value or desirability. These rules regarding what information must be disclosed, and whether the information must be disclosed even if a buyer does not ask, vary from one jurisdiction to the next.

a. Help desk and incident reporting auditing
b. Corporate Bond
c. Starving the beast
d. Disclosure

35. The term _____ describes a reduction in recognized value. In accounting terminology, it refers to recognition of the reduced or zero value of an asset. In income tax statements, it refers to a reduction of taxable income as recognition of certain expenses required to produce the income.

a. Current asset
b. Payroll
c. Salvage value
d. Write-off

36. In financial accounting, a _____ or statement of financial position is a summary of a person's or organization's balances. Assets, liabilities and ownership equity are listed as of a specific date, such as the end of its financial year. A _____ is often described as a snapshot of a company's financial condition.

a. Notes to the financial statements
b. Statement of retained earnings
c. 3M Company
d. Balance sheet

37. _____ is the ratio of sales (on the Profit and loss account) to the value of fixed assets (on the balance sheet.) It indicates how well the business is using its fixed assets to generate sales.

$$Fixed\ Asset\ Turnover = \frac{Sales}{Average\ net\ fixed\ assets}$$

Generally speaking, the higher the ratio, the better, because a high ratio indicates the business has less money tied up in fixed assets for each dollar of sales revenue.

   a. Defined benefit pension plan
   b. BMC Software, Inc.
   c. 3M Company
   d. Fixed asset turnover

38. The term '_____' refers to the concept of collecting information and attempting to spot a pattern in the information. In some fields of study, the term '_____' has more formally-defined meanings.

In project management _____ is a mathematical technique that uses historical results to predict future outcome.

   a. Multicollinearity
   b. 3M Company
   c. Regression analysis
   d. Trend analysis

39. In finance, the _____ or quick ratio or liquid ratio measures the ability of a company to use its near cash or quick assets to immediately extinguish or retire its current liabilities. Quick assets include those current assets that presumably can be quickly converted to cash at close to their book values.

$$Quick\ (Acid\ Test)\ Ratio = \frac{Cash + Marketable\ Securities + Accounts\ Receivables}{Current\ Liabilities}$$

Generally, the acid test ratio should be 1:1 or better, however this varies widely by industry.

   a. Invested capital
   b. Inventory turnover
   c. Earnings per share
   d. Acid-test

40. _____ is a financial ratio that measures the efficiency of a company's use of its assets in generating sales revenue or sales income to the company.

$$Asset\ Turnover = \frac{Sales}{Average Total Assets}$$

- 'Sales' is the value of 'Net Sales' or 'Sales' from the company's income statement
- 'Average Total Assets' is the value of 'Total assets' from the company's balance sheet in the beginning and the end of the fiscal period divided by 2.

   a. Enterprise Value/Sales
   b. Information ratio
   c. Asset turnover
   d. Average propensity to consume

Chapter 10. Current Liabilities and Payroll

1. _____ is a file or account that contains money that a person or company owes to suppliers, but has not paid yet (a form of debt.) When you receive an invoice you add it to the file, and then you remove it when you pay. Thus, the A/P is a form of credit that suppliers offer to their purchasers by allowing them to pay for a product or service after it has already been received.
   - a. Accounts receivable
   - b. Accrual
   - c. Earnings before interest, taxes, depreciation and amortization
   - d. Accounts payable

2. In finance, a _____ is the party in a loan agreement which receives money or other instrument from a lender and promises to repay the lender in a specified time.
   - a. Borrower
   - b. Simple interest
   - c. BMC Software, Inc.
   - d. 3M Company

3. A _____ is a party (e.g. person, organization, company, or government) that has a claim to the services of a second party. It is a person or institution to whom money is owed. The first party, in general, has provided some property or service to the second party under the assumption (usually enforced by contract) that the second party will return an equivalent property or service.
   - a. Cash and cash equivalents
   - b. Debtor
   - c. Creditor
   - d. Net worth

4. In accounting, _____ are considered liabilities of the business that are to be settled in cash within the fiscal year or the operating cycle, whichever period is longer.

   For example accounts payable for goods, services or supplies that were purchased for use in the operation of the business and payable within a normal period of time would be _____.

   Bonds, mortgages and loans that are payable over a term exceeding one year would be fixed liabilities.
   - a. Payroll
   - b. Treasury stock
   - c. Closing entries
   - d. Current liabilities

5. In economics a _____ is an entity that owes a debt to someone else. The entity may be an individual, a firm, a government, a company or other legal person. The counterparty is called a creditor.
   - a. Fair market value
   - b. Securitization
   - c. Money market
   - d. Debtor

6. A loan is a type of debt. Like all debt instruments, a loan entails the redistribution of financial assets over time, between the _____ and the borrower.

   In a loan, the borrower initially receives or borrows an amount of money, called the principal, from the _____, and is obligated to pay back or repay an equal amount of money to the _____ at a later time.
   - a. Loan to value
   - b. Credit rating
   - c. Debenture
   - d. Lender

Chapter 10. Current Liabilities and Payroll

7. In financial accounting, a _____ is defined as an obligation of an entity arising from past transactions or events, the settlement of which may result in the transfer or use of assets, provision of services or other yielding of economic benefits in the future.
   - a. Trust Indenture Act of 1939
   - b. Pre-emption right
   - c. Resource Conservation and Recovery Act
   - d. Liability

8. In economic models, the _____ time frame assumes no fixed factors of production. Firms can enter or leave the marketplace, and the cost (and availability) of land, labor, raw materials, and capital goods can be assumed to vary. In contrast, in the short-run time frame, certain factors are assumed to be fixed, because there is not sufficient time for them to change.
   - a. BMC Software, Inc.
   - b. Long-run
   - c. Short-run
   - d. 3M Company

9. _____ are liabilities with a future benefit over one year, such as notes payable that mature greater than one year.

   In accounting, the _____ are shown on the right wing of the balance-sheet representing the sources of funds, which are generally bounded in form of capital assets.

   Examples of _____ are debentures, mortgage loans and other bank loans (note: not all bank loans are long term as not all are paid over a period greater than a year, the example is bridging loan.)

   - a. Long-term liabilities
   - b. Gross sales
   - c. Cash basis accounting
   - d. Book value

10. _____ is that which is owed; usually referencing assets owed, but the term can also cover moral obligations and other interactions not requiring money. In the case of assets, _____ is a means of using future purchasing power in the present before a summation has been earned. Some companies and corporations use _____ as a part of their overall corporate finance strategy.
    - a. Loan
    - b. Lender
    - c. Debenture
    - d. Debt

11. A _____, also referred to as a note payable in accounting, is a contract where one party (the maker or issuer) makes an unconditional promise in writing to pay a sum of money to the other (the payee), either at a fixed or determinable future time or on demand of the payee, under specific terms. They differ from IOUs in that they contain a specific promise to pay, rather than simply acknowledging that a debt exists.

    The terms of a note typically include the principal amount, the interest rate if any, and the maturity date.

    - a. Promissory note
    - b. BNSF Railway
    - c. 3M Company
    - d. BMC Software, Inc.

12. In economics, the concept of the _____ refers to the decision-making time frame of a firm in which at least one factor of production is fixed. Costs which are fixed in the _____ have no impact on a firms decisions. For example a firm can raise output by increasing the amount of labour through overtime.

a. Short-run
c. 3M Company
b. Long-run
d. BMC Software, Inc.

13. Discounting is a financial mechanism in which a debtor obtains the right to delay payments to a creditor, for a defined period of time, in exchange for a charge or fee. Essentially, the party that owes money in the present purchases the right to delay the payment until some future date. The _____, or charge, is simply the difference between the original amount owed in the present and the amount that has to be paid in the future to settle the debt.

a. Risk aversion
c. Risk
b. Discount
d. Risk adjusted return on capital

14. The _____ is an interest rate a central bank charges depository institutions that borrow reserves from it.

The term _____ has two meanings:

- the same as interest rate; the term 'discount' does not refer to the meaning of the word, but to the purpose of using the quantity, such as computations of present value, e.g. net present value or discounted cash flow

- the annual effective _____, which is the annual interest divided by the capital including that interest; this rate is lower than the interest rate; it corresponds to using the value after a year as the nominal value, and seeing the initial value as the nominal value minus a discount; it is used for Treasury Bills and similar financial instruments

The annual effective _____ is the annual interest divided by the capital including that interest, which is the interest rate divided by 100% plus the interest rate. It is the annual discount factor to be applied to the future cash flow, to find the discount, subtracted from a future value to find the value one year earlier.

For example, suppose there is a government bond that sells for $95 and pays $100 in a year's time.

a. Convertible bond
c. Municipal bond
b. Process time
d. Discount rate

15. The _____ is an executive department and the treasury of the United States federal government. It was established by an Act of Congress in 1789 to manage government revenue. The Department is administered by the Secretary of the Treasury, who is a member of the Cabinet.

a. Debt-to-GDP ratios
c. Factor
b. Department of the Treasury
d. Screening

16. _____ is the process of increasing, or accounting for, an amount over a period of time. Particular instances of the term include:

- _____, the allocation of a lump sum amount to different time periods, particularly for loans and other forms of finance, including related interest or other finance charges.
    - _____ schedule, a table detailing each periodic payment on a loan (typically a mortgage), as generated by an _____ calculator.
    - Negative _____, an _____ schedule where the loan amount actually increases through not paying the full interest
- Amortized analysis, analyzing the execution cost of algorithms over a sequence of operations.
- _____ of capital expenditures of certain assets under accounting rules, particularly intangible assets, in a manner analogous to depreciation.
- _____

a. Amortization
b. Annuity
c. EBIT
d. Intangible

17. In finance, a _____ is a debt security, in which the authorized issuer owes the holders a debt and, depending on the terms of the _____, is obliged to pay interest (the coupon) and/or to repay the principal at a later date, termed maturity. It is a formal contract to repay borrowed money with interest at fixed intervals.

Thus a _____ is like a loan: the issuer is the borrower, the _____ holder is the lender, and the coupon is the interest.

a. Zero-coupon bond
b. Revenue bonds
c. Coupon rate
d. Bond

18. _____ is a fee paid on borrowed assets. It is the price paid for the use of borrowed money , or, money earned by deposited funds .Assets that are sometimes lent with _____ include money, shares, consumer goods through hire purchase, major assets such as aircraft, and even entire factories in finance lease arrangements. The _____ is calculated upon the value of the assets in the same manner as upon money.

a. ABC Television Network
b. Insolvency
c. AIG
d. Interest

19. In a company, _____ is the sum of all financial records of salaries, wages, bonuses and deductions.

A paycheck, is traditionally a paper document issued by an employer to pay an employee for services rendered. While most commonly used in the United States, recently the physical paycheck has been increasingly replaced by electronic direct deposit to bank accounts.

a. Total Expense Ratio
b. 3M Company
c. Tax expense
d. Payroll

20. _____ generally refers to two kinds of taxes: Taxes which employers are required to withhold from employees' pay Pay-As-You-Earn or Pay-As-You-Go tax; and taxes which are paid from the employer's own funds and which are directly related to employing a worker, which may be either fixed charges or proportionally linked to an employee's pay.

Chapter 10. Current Liabilities and Payroll

In Australia, the _____ is a specific tax which is paid to states and territories by employers, not by employees. The tax is not deducted from the worker's pay.

a. Federal Insurance Contributions Act
b. Tax refund
c. State tax levels
d. Payroll tax

21. In economics, business, retail, and accounting, a _____ is the value of money that has been used up to produce something, and hence is not available for use anymore. In economics, a _____ is an alternative that is given up as a result of a decision. In business, the _____ may be one of acquisition, in which case the amount of money expended to acquire it is counted as _____.

a. Prime cost
b. Cost of quality
c. Cost allocation
d. Cost

22. _____ is a specific term used in companies' financial reporting from the company-whole point of view. Because that use excludes the effects of changing ownership interest, an economic measure of _____ is necessary for financial analysis from the shareholders' point of view

_____ is defined by the Financial Accounting Standards Board, or FASB, as 'the change in equity [net assets] of a business enterprise during a period from transactions and other events and circumstances from nonowner sources. It includes all changes in equity during a period except those resulting from investments by owners and distributions to owners.'

_____ is the sum of net income and other items that must bypass the income statement because they have not been realized, including items like an unrealized holding gain or loss from available for sale securities and foreign currency translation gains or losses.

a. 3M Company
b. BNSF Railway
c. BMC Software, Inc.
d. Comprehensive income

23. _____ is a private company with headquarters in Redmond, Washington. It has offices in Redmond, Bellingham, Vancouver, Washington; Newport Beach, California, Washington, DC, and London.

_____ provides competitive salary levels for non-profit and for-profit corporations for any of over 5000 job titles.

a. AMEX
b. ABC Television Network
c. Economic Research Institute
d. AIG

24. Employment is a contract between two parties, one being the employer and the other being the _____. An _____ may be defined as: 'A person in the service of another under any contract of hire, express or implied, oral or written, where the employer has the power or right to control and direct the _____ in the material details of how the work is to be performed.' Black's Law Dictionary page 471 (5th ed. 1979.)

a. ABC Television Network
b. AIG
c. AMEX
d. Employee

Chapter 10. Current Liabilities and Payroll

25. The _____ of 1938 (_____, ch. 676, 52 Stat. 1060, June 25, 1938, 29 U.S.C.
    a. Joint venture
    b. Property
    c. Fair Labor Standards Act
    d. Sarbanes-Oxley Act

26. The _____ is a United States federal law that imposes a federal employer tax used to fund state workforce agencies. Employers report this tax by filing an annual Form 940 with the Internal Revenue Service.
    a. FUTA
    b. Tax exemption
    c. Federal Unemployment Tax Act
    d. Laffer curve

27. A _____ is a form of periodic payment from an employer to an employee, which may be specified in an employment contract. It is contrasted with piece wages, where each job, hour or other unit is paid separately, rather than on a periodic basis.

From the point of a view of running a business, _____ can also be viewed as the cost of acquiring human resources for running operations, and is then termed personnel expense or _____ expense.

   a. Separation of duties
   b. BMC Software, Inc.
   c. Salary
   d. 3M Company

28. An _____ is a tax levied on the financial income of people, corporations, or other legal entities. Various _____ systems exist, with varying degrees of tax incidence. Income taxation can be progressive, proportional, or regressive.
    a. Income tax
    b. Implied level of government service
    c. Individual Retirement Arrangement
    d. Ordinary income

29. _____ is the remaining amount after deductions from the gross salary, where net means ultimate.

Example deductions: income taxes, trade union dues, authorized deduction for a retirement fund.

_____ is the amount left over after deductions from the gross salary.

   a. Residual value
   b. Round-tripping
   c. 3M Company
   d. Net pay

30. A _____ is a compensation, usually financial, received by a worker in exchange for their labor.

Compensation in terms of _____s is given to worker and compensation in terms of salary is given to employees. Compensation is a monetary benefits given to employees in returns of the services provided by them.

   a. Retirement plan
   b. 3M Company
   c. BMC Software, Inc.
   d. Wage

31. According to the Gregorian calendar, the _____ begins on January 1 and ends on December 31.

Chapter 10. Current Liabilities and Payroll

Generally speaking, a _____ begins on the New Year's Day of the given calendar system and ends on the day before the following New Year's Day. In the Gregorian calendar, this is normally 365 days, but 366 days in a leap year, giving an average length of 365.2425 days.

a. BMC Software, Inc.
b. Calendar year
c. BNSF Railway
d. 3M Company

32. _____ in the United States currently refers to the federal Old-Age, Survivors, and Disability Insurance (OASDI) program.

The original _____ Act and the current version of the Act, as amended encompass several social welfare and social insurance programs. The larger and better known programs are:

- Federal Old-Age, Survivors, and Disability Insurance
- Unemployment benefits
- Temporary Assistance for Needy Families
- Health Insurance for Aged and Disabled (Medicare)
- Grants to States for Medical Assistance Programs (Medicaid)
- State Children's Health Insurance Program (SCHIP)
- Supplemental Security Income (Social Securityl)

U.S. _____ is a social insurance program funded through dedicated payroll taxes called Federal Insurance Contributions Act (FICA.) Tax deposits are formally entrusted to Federal Old-Age and Survivors Insurance Trust Fund, or Federal Disability Insurance Trust Fund, Federal Hospital Insurance Trust Fund or the Federal Supplementary Medical Insurance Trust Fund.

a. Social security
b. Yield
c. Factor
d. Tertiary sector of economy

33. A _____ is a fungible, negotiable instrument representing financial value. they are broadly categorized into debt securities (such as banknotes, bonds and debentures), and equity securities; e.g., common stocks. The company or other entity issuing the _____ is called the issuer.

a. Tracking stock
b. Security
c. BMC Software, Inc.
d. 3M Company

34. The _____ (or _____, 26 U.S.C. ch.23) is a United States federal law that imposes a federal employer tax used to fund state workforce agencies. Employers report this tax by filing an annual Form 940 with the Internal Revenue Service.

a. Golsen v. Commissioner of Internal Revenue
b. Direct tax
c. Natural resources consumption tax
d. FUTA

35. A _____ is the transfer of wealth from one party (such as a person or company) to another. A _____ is usually made in exchange for the provision of goods, services or both, or to fulfill a legal obligation.

The simplest and oldest form of _____ is barter, the exchange of one good or service for another.

a. Payee
b. 3M Company
c. BMC Software, Inc.
d. Payment

36. _____ refers to fraudulent or deceptive activity or representation on the part of an employee or prospective employee toward an employer. It is not to be confused with employment fraud, in which a posing employer scams one who is seeking a job or else fails to pay wages for work performed. There are several types of _____s that employees or potential employees have been known to commit against employers.

a. North American Free Trade Agreement
b. Job fraud
c. Carbon offset
d. Chief executive officer

37. The term _____ refers to government debt, expenditures and revenues, or to finance (particularly financial revenue) in general.

- _____ deficit is the budget deficit of federal or local government
- _____ policy is the discretionary spending of governments. Contrasts with monetary policy.
- _____ year and _____ quarter are reporting periods for firms and other agencies.

See also

- Procurator _____ and Crown Office and Procurator _____ Service

a. General partner
b. Homogeneous
c. Fiscal
d. Tertiary sector of economy

38. A _____ is a period used for calculating annual financial statements in businesses and other organizations. In many jurisdictions, regulatory laws regarding accounting and taxation require such reports once per twelve months, but do not require that the period reported on constitutes a calendar year (i.e., January through December.) _____s vary between businesses and countries.

a. BMC Software, Inc.
b. 3M Company
c. BNSF Railway
d. Fiscal year

39. An _____ is a term used in behavioral economics to describe those types of behaviors that impose costs on a person in the long-run that are not taken into account when making decisions in the present. Classical Economics discourages government from creating legislation that targets internalities, because it is assumed that the consumer takes these personal costs into account when paying for the good that causes the _____. For example, cigarettes should be taxed because of the negative consumption externalities that they impose, such as second-hand smoke, not because the smoker harms him or herself by smoking.

a. Authorised capital
b. Operating budget
c. Inventory turnover ratio
d. Internality

40. In accounting and organizational theory, _____ is defined as a process effected by an organization's structure, work and authority flows, people and management information systems, designed to help the organization accomplish specific goals or objectives. It is a means by which an organization's resources are directed, monitored, and measured. It plays an important role in preventing and detecting fraud and protecting the organization's resources, both physical (e.g., machinery and property) and intangible (e.g., reputation or intellectual property such as trademarks.)
   a. Audit committee
   b. Internal control
   c. Audit risk
   d. Auditor independence

41. _____ and benefits in kind are various non-wage compensations provided to employees in addition to their normal wages or salaries. Where an employee exchanges (cash) wages for some other form of benefit, this is generally referred to as a 'salary sacrifice' arrangement. In most countries, most kinds of _____ are taxable to at least some degree.
   a. ABC Television Network
   b. AIG
   c. AMEX
   d. Employee benefits

42. In economics, a _____ is a type of pension plan in which an employer promises a specified monthly benefit on retirement that is predetermined by a formula based on the employee's earnings history, tenure of service and age, rather than depending on investment returns. It is 'defined' in the sense that the formula for computing the employer's contribution is known in advance. In the United States, 26 U.S.C.
   a. 3M Company
   b. Defined benefit pension plan
   c. BMC Software, Inc.
   d. Fixed asset turnover

43. _____ that may or may not be incurred by an entity depending on the outcome of a future event such as a court case. These liabilities are recorded in a company's accounts and shown in the balance sheet when both probable and reasonably estimable. A footnote to the balance sheet describes the nature and extent of the _____.
   a. Headnote
   b. Nonacquiescence
   c. Tangible
   d. Contingent liabilities

44. The term _____ or superannuation refers to a pension granted upon retirement. They may be set up by employers, insurance companies, the government or other institutions such as employer associations or trade unions.
   a. Wage
   b. BMC Software, Inc.
   c. 3M Company
   d. Retirement plan

45. In finance, the _____ or quick ratio or liquid ratio measures the ability of a company to use its near cash or quick assets to immediately extinguish or retire its current liabilities. Quick assets include those current assets that presumably can be quickly converted to cash at close to their book values.

$$\text{Quick (Acid Test) Ratio} = \frac{\text{Cash} + \text{Marketable Securities} + \text{Accounts Receivables}}{\text{Current Liabilities}}$$

Generally, the acid test ratio should be 1:1 or better, however this varies widely by industry.

   a. Earnings per share
   b. Inventory turnover
   c. Invested capital
   d. Acid-test

46. In business and accounting, _____ are everything of value that is owned by a person or company. It is a claim on the property your income of a borrower. The balance sheet of a firm records the monetary value of the _____ owned by the firm.

a. Accounts receivable

b. Earnings before interest, taxes, depreciation and amortization

c. Accrual basis accounting

d. Assets

Chapter 11. Corporations: Organization, Stock Transactions, and Dividends

1. In financial accounting, a _____ is defined as an obligation of an entity arising from past transactions or events, the settlement of which may result in the transfer or use of assets, provision of services or other yielding of economic benefits in the future.
   a. Resource Conservation and Recovery Act
   b. Trust Indenture Act of 1939
   c. Pre-emption right
   d. Liability

2. _____ is a concept whereby a person's financial liability is limited to a fixed sum, most commonly the value of a person's investment in a company or partnership with _____. A shareholder in a limited company is not personally liable for any of the debts of the company, other than for the value of his investment in that company. The same is true for the members of a _____ partnership and the limited partners in a limited partnership.
   a. Burden of proof
   b. Sumptuary
   c. Staple right
   d. Limited liability

3. The term _____ usually refers to a company that is permitted to offer its registered securities (stock, bonds, etc.) for sale to the general public, typically through a stock exchange, or occasionally a company whose stock is traded over the counter (OTC) via market makers who use non-exchange quotation services.

   The term '_____' may also refer to a company owned by the government.

   a. Privately held
   b. National Conference of Commissioners on Uniform State Laws
   c. MicroStrategy
   d. Public company

4. A mutual shareholder or _____ is an individual or company (including a corporation) that legally owns one or more shares of stock in a joint stock company. A company's shareholders collectively own that company. Thus, the typical goal of such companies is to enhance shareholder value.
   a. Stock split
   b. 3M Company
   c. Growth investing
   d. Stockholder

5. _____ is typically a 'higher ranking' stock than voting shares, and its terms are negotiated between the corporation and the investor.

   _____ usually carries no voting rights, but may carry superior priority over common stock in the payment of dividends and upon liquidation. _____ may carry a dividend that is paid out prior to any dividends being paid to common stock holders.

   a. Public offering
   b. Restricted stock
   c. Preferred Stock
   d. Flow-through entity

6. A _____ is a body of elected or appointed members who jointly oversee the activities of a company or organization. The body sometimes has a different name, such as board of trustees, board of governors, board of managers, or executive board. It is often simply referred to as 'the board.'

A board's activities are determined by the powers, duties, and responsibilities delegated to it or conferred on it by an authority outside itself.

Chapter 11. Corporations: Organization, Stock Transactions, and Dividends

a. Pre-emption right
b. FLSA
c. Board of directors
d. Fair Labor Standards Act

7. _____ are payments made by a corporation to its shareholder members. It is the portion of corporate profits paid out to stockholders. When a corporation earns a profit or surplus, that money can be put to two uses: it can either be re-invested in the business (called retained earnings), or it can be paid to the shareholders as a dividend.

a. Dividend stripping
b. Franking credit
c. Dividend payout ratio
d. Dividends

8. _____ is the imposition of two or more taxes on the same income (in the case of income taxes), asset (in the case of capital taxes), or financial transaction (in the case of sales taxes.) It refers to two distinct situations:

- taxation of dividend income without relief or credit for taxes paid by the company paying the dividend on the income from which the dividend is paid. This arises in the so-called 'classical' system of corporate taxation, used in the United States.
- taxation by two or more countries of the same income, asset or transaction, for example income paid by an entity of one country to a resident of a different country. The double liability is often mitigated by tax treaties between countries.

It is not unusual for a business or individual who is resident in one country to make a taxable gain (earnings, profits) in another. This person may find that he is obliged by domestic laws to pay tax on that gain locally and pay again in the country in which the gain was made. Since this is inequitable, many nations make bilateral _____ agreements with each other.

a. Windfall profits tax
b. Tax avoidance and tax evasion
c. Regressive tax
d. Double taxation

9. An _____ is a mostly hierarchical concept of subordination of entities that collaborate and contribute to serve one common aim.

Organizations are a variant of clustered entities. The structure of an organization is usually set up in many a styles, dependent on their objectives and ambience.

a. AMEX
b. AIG
c. ABC Television Network
d. Organizational structure

10. The _____ are the primary rules governing the management of a corporation in the United States and Canada, and are filed with a state or other regulatory agency. The equivalent in the United Kingdom and various other countries is Articles of Association.

Chapter 11. Corporations: Organization, Stock Transactions, and Dividends

A corporation's _____ generally provide information such as:

- The corporation's name, which has to be unique from any other corporation in that jurisdiction. As part of the corporation's name, certain words such as 'incorporated', 'limited', 'corporation', (or their abbreviations) or some equivalent term in countries whose language is not English, are usually required as part of the name as a 'flag' to indicate to persons doing business with the organization that it is a corporation as opposed to an individual or partnership (with unlimited liability.) In some cases, certain types of names are prohibited except by special permission, such as words implying the corporation is a government agency or has powers to act in ways it is not otherwise allowed.
- The name of the person(s) organizing the corporation (usually members of the board of directors.)
- Whether the corporation is a stock corporation or a non-stock corporation.
- Whether the corporation's existence is permanent or limited for a specific period of time. Generally the rule is that a corporation existence is forever, or until (1) it stops paying the yearly corporate renewal fees or otherwise fails to do something required to continue its existence such as file certain paperwork each year; or (2) it files a request to 'wind up and dissolve.'
- In some cases, a corporation must state the purposes for which it is formed. Some jurisdictions permit a general statement such as 'any lawful purpose' but some require explicit specifications.
- If a non-stock corporation, whether it is for profit or non-profit. However, some jurisdictions differentiate by 'for profit' or 'non profit' and some by 'stock or non-stock'.
- In the United States, if a corporation is to be organized as a non-profit, to be recognized as such by the Internal Revenue Service, such as for eligibility for tax exemption, certain specific wording must be included stating no part of the assets of the corporation are to benefit the members.
- If a stock corporation, the number of shares the corporation is authorized to issue, or the maximum amount in a specific currency of stock that may be issued, e.g. a maximum of $25,000.
- The number and names of the corporation's initial Board of Directors (though this is optional in most cases.)
- The initial director(s) of the corporation (in some cases the incorporator or the registered agent must be a director, if not an attorney or another corporation.)
- The location of the corporation's 'registered office' - the location at which legal papers can be served to the corporation if necessary. Some states further require the designation of a Registered Agent: a person to whom such papers could be delivered.

Most states permit a corporation to be formed by one person; in some cases (such as non-profit corporations) it may require three or five or more. This change has come about as a result of Delaware liberalizing its corporation rules to allow corporations to be formed by one person, and states not wanting to lose corporate charters to Delaware had to revise their rules as a result.

a. Exclusive right
c. Articles of incorporation
b. Employee Retirement Income Security Act
d. Express warranty

11. _____ can refer to a law of local or limited application, passed under the authority of a higher law specifying what things may be regulated by the _____, or it can refer to the internal rules of a company or organisation.

a. Bylaw
b. Fraud Enforcement and Recovery Act
c. FLSA
d. Consumer protection laws

12. A _____ is the grant of authority or rights, stating that the granter formally recognizes the prerogative of the recipient to exercise the rights specified. It is implicit that the granter retains superiority (or sovereignty), and that the recipient admits a limited (or inferior) status within the relationship, and it is within that sense that _____s were historically granted, and that sense is retained in modern usage of the term. Also, _____ can simply be a document giving royal permission to start a colony.
   a. Recharacterisation
   b. Tax patent
   c. Chief Financial Officers Act of 1990
   d. Charter

13. The _____ of 2002 (Pub.L. 107-204, 116 Stat. 745, enacted July 30, 2002), also known as the Public Company Accounting Reform and Investor Protection Act of 2002, is a United States federal law enacted on July 30, 2002 in response to a number of major corporate and accounting scandals including those affecting Enron, Tyco International, Adelphia, Peregrine Systems and WorldCom. The legislation establishes new or enhanced standards for all U.S. public company boards, management, and public accounting firms. It does not apply to privately held companies.
   a. Burden of proof
   b. Staple right
   c. Tax lien
   d. Sarbanes-Oxley Act

14. In economics, _____ or _____ goods or real _____ refers to factors of production used to create goods or services that are not themselves significantly consumed (though they may depreciate) in the production process. _____ goods may be acquired with money or financial _____. In finance and accounting, _____ generally refers to financial wealth, especially that used to start or maintain a business.
   a. Sale
   b. Debt-to-GDP ratios
   c. Capital
   d. Consumption

15. _____ are common shares that have been authorized, issued, and purchased by investors. They have voting rights and represent ownership in the corporation by the person or institution that holds the shares. They should be distinguished from treasury shares, which are common stock repurchased by the corporation.
   a. Preferred stock
   b. Controlling interest
   c. Participating preferred stock
   d. Shares outstanding

16. In corporate law, a _____ is a legal document that certifies ownership of a specific number of stock shares in a corporation. In large corporations, buying shares does not always lead to a _____

Usually only shareholders with _____s can vote in a shareholders' general meeting.

   a. BNSF Railway
   b. BMC Software, Inc.
   c. 3M Company
   d. Stock certificate

17. The _____ is a United States federal law that imposes a federal employer tax used to fund state workforce agencies. Employers report this tax by filing an annual Form 940 with the Internal Revenue Service.
   a. Laffer curve
   b. FUTA
   c. Tax exemption
   d. Federal Unemployment Tax Act

Chapter 11. Corporations: Organization, Stock Transactions, and Dividends

18. _____ is a form of corporation equity ownership represented in the securities. It is a stock whose dividends are based on market fluctuations. It is dangerous in comparison to preferred shares and some other investment options, in that in the event of bankruptcy, _____ investors receive their funds after preferred stock holders, bondholders, creditors, etc. On the other hand, common shares on average perform better than preferred shares or bonds over time.
    a. 3M Company
    b. Growth investing
    c. Stock split
    d. Common stock

19. A _____ is the dividend paid to common stock owners from the profits of the company. Like other dividends, the payout is in the form of cash or other like stock. The law may regulate the size of the _____ particularly when the payout is a cash distribution tantamount to a liquidation.
    a. Tax patent
    b. Types of business
    c. Due diligence
    d. Common stock dividend

20. _____ is capital stock which provides a specific dividend that is paid before any dividends are paid to common stock holders, and which takes precedence over common stock in the event of a liquidation. This form of financing is used by private equity investors and venture capital firms. Holders of _____ get both their money back (with interest) and the money that is distributable with respect to the percentage of common shares into which their preferred stock can convert.
    a. Participating preferred stock
    b. Commercial paper
    c. Gross profit margin
    d. Cash flow

21. Discounting is a financial mechanism in which a debtor obtains the right to delay payments to a creditor, for a defined period of time, in exchange for a charge or fee. Essentially, the party that owes money in the present purchases the right to delay the payment until some future date. The _____, or charge, is simply the difference between the original amount owed in the present and the amount that has to be paid in the future to settle the debt.
    a. Risk adjusted return on capital
    b. Risk
    c. Risk aversion
    d. Discount

22. Companies that have publicly traded securities typically use _____s to keep track of the individuals and entities that own their stocks and bonds. Most _____s are banks or trust companies, but sometimes a company acts as its own _____.

    _____s perform three main functions:

    1. Issue and cancel certificates to reflect changes in ownership. For example, when a company declares a stock dividend or stock split, the _____ issues new shares. _____s keep records of who owns a company's stocks and bonds and how those stocks and bonds are held--whether by the owner in certificate form, by the company in book-entry form, or by the investor's brokerage firm in street name. They also keep records of how many shares or bonds each investor owns.
    2. Act as an intermediary for the company. A _____ may also serve as the company's paying agent to pay out interest, cash and stock dividends, or other distributions to stock- and bondholders. In addition, _____s act as proxy agent (sending out proxy materials), exchange agent (exchanging a company's stock or bonds in a merger), tender agent (tendering shares in a tender offer), and mailing agent (mailing the company's quarterly, annual, and other reports.)
    3. Handle lost, destroyed, or stolen certificates. _____s help shareholders and bondholders when a stock or bond certificate has been lost, destroyed, or stolen.

Chapter 11. Corporations: Organization, Stock Transactions, and Dividends

In many cases, you can find out which _____ a company uses by visiting the investor relations section of the companye;s website.

a. Mark-to-market
c. Financial market
b. Transfer agent
d. Market price

23. _____ is the process of increasing, or accounting for, an amount over a period of time. Particular instances of the term include:

- _____, the allocation of a lump sum amount to different time periods, particularly for loans and other forms of finance, including related interest or other finance charges.
    - _____ schedule, a table detailing each periodic payment on a loan (typically a mortgage), as generated by an _____ calculator.
    - Negative _____, an _____ schedule where the loan amount actually increases through not paying the full interest
- Amortized analysis, analyzing the execution cost of algorithms over a sequence of operations.
- _____ of capital expenditures of certain assets under accounting rules, particularly intangible assets, in a manner analogous to depreciation.
- _____

a. Intangible
c. Amortization
b. Annuity
d. EBIT

24. In finance, a _____ is a debt security, in which the authorized issuer owes the holders a debt and, depending on the terms of the _____, is obliged to pay interest (the coupon) and/or to repay the principal at a later date, termed maturity. It is a formal contract to repay borrowed money with interest at fixed intervals.

Thus a _____ is like a loan: the issuer is the borrower, the _____ holder is the lender, and the coupon is the interest.

a. Revenue bonds
c. Bond
b. Coupon rate
d. Zero-coupon bond

25. _____ is a fee paid on borrowed assets. It is the price paid for the use of borrowed money , or, money earned by deposited funds .Assets that are sometimes lent with _____ include money, shares, consumer goods through hire purchase, major assets such as aircraft, and even entire factories in finance lease arrangements. The _____ is calculated upon the value of the assets in the same manner as upon money.

a. AIG
c. ABC Television Network
b. Insolvency
d. Interest

26. _____ is a payment of a dividend to stockholders that exceeds the company's retained earnings. Once retained earnings is depleted, capital accounts such as additional paid-in capital are decreased to make up for the remaining dividend to be paid to stockholders. When a _____ occurs, it is considered to be a return of investment instead of profits.

a. Fund accounting
c. Redemption value
b. Liquidating dividend
d. Trade name

27. A _____ is the transfer of wealth from one party (such as a person or company) to another. A _____ is usually made in exchange for the provision of goods, services or both, or to fulfill a legal obligation.

The simplest and oldest form of _____ is barter, the exchange of one good or service for another.

a. Payee
c. BMC Software, Inc.
b. 3M Company
d. Payment

28. _____, also called fair price (in a commonplace conflation of the two distinct concepts), is a concept used in finance and economics, defined as a rational and unbiased estimate of the potential market price of a good, service, or asset, taking into account such objective factors as:

- acquisition/production/distribution costs, replacement costs, or costs of close substitutes
- actual utility at a given level of development of social productive capability
- supply vs. demand

and subjective factors such as

- risk characteristics
- cost of capital
- individually perceived utility

In accounting, _____ is used as an estimate of the market value of an asset (or liability) for which a market price cannot be determined (usually because there is no established market for the asset.) Under GAAP (FAS 157), _____ is the amount at which the asset could be bought or sold in a current transaction between willing parties, or transferred to an equivalent party, other than in a liquidation sale. This is used for assets whose carrying value is based on mark-to-market valuations; for assets carried at historical cost, the _____ of the asset is not used. One example of where _____ is an issue is a College kitchen with a cost of $2 million which was built 5 years ago.

a. 3M Company
c. Fair value
b. BNSF Railway
d. BMC Software, Inc.

29. In economics, business, retail, and accounting, a _____ is the value of money that has been used up to produce something, and hence is not available for use anymore. In economics, a _____ is an alternative that is given up as a result of a decision. In business, the _____ may be one of acquisition, in which case the amount of money expended to acquire it is counted as _____.

a. Cost allocation
c. Cost of quality
b. Prime cost
d. Cost

30. A _____ or reacquired stock is stock which is bought back by the issuing company, reducing the amount of outstanding stock on the open market ('open market' including insiders' holdings).

Chapter 11. Corporations: Organization, Stock Transactions, and Dividends

Stock repurchases are often used as a tax-efficient method to put cash into shareholders' hands, rather than pay dividends. Sometimes, companies do this when they feel that their stock is undervalued on the open market.

a. Matching principle
b. Treasury stock
c. Cost of goods sold
d. Net profit

31. The term '_____' refers to the concept of collecting information and attempting to spot a pattern in the information. In some fields of study, the term '_____' has more formally-defined meanings.

In project management _____ is a mathematical technique that uses historical results to predict future outcome.

a. 3M Company
b. Regression analysis
c. Trend analysis
d. Multicollinearity

32. In financial accounting, a _____ or statement of financial position is a summary of a person's or organization's balances. Assets, liabilities and ownership equity are listed as of a specific date, such as the end of its financial year. A _____ is often described as a snapshot of a company's financial condition.

a. Balance sheet
b. Notes to the financial statements
c. Statement of retained earnings
d. 3M Company

33. The _____ is one of the basic financial statements as per Generally Accepted Accounting Principles, and it explains the changes in a company's retained earnings over the reporting period. It breaks down changes affecting the account, such as profits or losses from operations, dividends paid, and any other items charged or credited to retained earnings. A retained earnings statement is required by Generally Accepted Accounting Principles whenever comparative balance sheets and income statements are presented.

a. Financial statements
b. Notes to the financial statements
c. Statement of retained earnings
d. 3M Company

34. _____ is a specific term used in companies' financial reporting from the company-whole point of view. Because that use excludes the effects of changing ownership interest, an economic measure of _____ is necessary for financial analysis from the shareholders' point of view

_____ is defined by the Financial Accounting Standards Board, or FASB, as 'the change in equity [net assets] of a business enterprise during a period from transactions and other events and circumstances from nonowner sources. It includes all changes in equity during a period except those resulting from investments by owners and distributions to owners.'

_____ is the sum of net income and other items that must bypass the income statement because they have not been realized, including items like an unrealized holding gain or loss from available for sale securities and foreign currency translation gains or losses.

a. BMC Software, Inc.
b. Comprehensive income
c. 3M Company
d. BNSF Railway

Chapter 11. Corporations: Organization, Stock Transactions, and Dividends

35. _____ is the act of taking possession of or assigning purpose to properties or ideas and is important in many topics, including:

- _____ in relation to the spread of knowledge
- _____ (art)
    - _____ (music) in reference to the re-use and proliferation of different types of music
- _____ (economics) origination of human ownership of previously unowned natural resources such as land
- _____ (law) as a component of government spending
- Cultural _____ is the borrowing, or theft, of an element of cultural expression of one group by another.
- The tort of _____ is one form of invasion of privacy.

a. Intangible
c. Annuity
b. Appropriation
d. Improvement

36. _____ is an asset, such as unpaid proceeds from a delivery of goods or services, at which such income item is earned and the related revenue item is recognized, while cash for them is to be received in a latter period, when its amount is deducted from the _____.

a. Assets
c. Accrued revenue
b. Accrued expense
d. Accounts receivable

37. In accounting, _____ has a very specific meaning. It is an outflow of cash or other valuable assets from a person or company to another person or company. This outflow of cash is generally one side of a trade for products or services that have equal or better current or future value to the buyer than to the seller.

a. AMEX
c. AIG
b. ABC Television Network
d. Expense

38. A _____ or stock divide increases or decreases the number of shares in a public company. The price is adjusted such that the before and after market capitalization of the company remains the same and dilution does not occur. Options and warrants are included.

a. Stockholder
c. 3M Company
b. Growth investing
d. Stock split

39. The _____ on a company stock is the company's annual dividend payments divided by its market cap, or the dividend per share divided by the price per share. It is often expressed as a percentage.

Dividend payments on preferred shares are stipulated by the prospectus.

a. Dividend stripping
c. Dividends
b. Dividend payout ratio
d. Dividend yield

40. In finance, the term _____ describes the amount in cash that returns to the owners of a security. Normally it does not include the price variations, at the difference of the total return. _____ applies to various stated rates of return on stocks (common and preferred, and convertible), fixed income instruments (bonds, notes, bills, strips, zero coupon), and some other investment type insurance products (e.g. annuities.)

a. Pension System
b. Capital
c. Yield
d. Corporate Bond

Chapter 12. Income Taxes, Unusual Income Items, and Investments in Stocks

1. An _____ is a tax levied on the financial income of people, corporations, or other legal entities. Various _____ systems exist, with varying degrees of tax incidence. Income taxation can be progressive, proportional, or regressive.

   a. Income tax
   b. Individual Retirement Arrangement
   c. Implied level of government service
   d. Ordinary income

2. In financial accounting, a _____ is defined as an obligation of an entity arising from past transactions or events, the settlement of which may result in the transfer or use of assets, provision of services or other yielding of economic benefits in the future.

   a. Trust Indenture Act of 1939
   b. Pre-emption right
   c. Resource Conservation and Recovery Act
   d. Liability

3. A _____ is the transfer of wealth from one party (such as a person or company) to another. A _____ is usually made in exchange for the provision of goods, services or both, or to fulfill a legal obligation.

   The simplest and oldest form of _____ is barter, the exchange of one good or service for another.

   a. Payee
   b. 3M Company
   c. BMC Software, Inc.
   d. Payment

4. In a company, _____ is the sum of all financial records of salaries, wages, bonuses and deductions.

   A paycheck, is traditionally a paper document issued by an employer to pay an employee for services rendered. While most commonly used in the United States, recently the physical paycheck has been increasingly replaced by electronic direct deposit to bank accounts.

   a. Tax expense
   b. 3M Company
   c. Total Expense Ratio
   d. Payroll

5. _____ is the portion of income that is the subject of taxation according to the laws that determine what is income and the taxation rate for that income. Generally, _____ refers to an individual's (or corporation's) gross income, adjusted for various deductions allowable by statute. The main questions put by most individuals in any jurisdiction are 'what makes up my _____' and what tax rates should be applied such that I can work out my tax liability to the state.

   a. Net operating loss
   b. Half-year convention
   c. Reverse Morris trust
   d. Taxable Income

6. The _____ is the current method of accelerated asset depreciation required by the United States income tax code. Under _____, all assets are divided into classes which dictate the number of years over which an asset's cost will be recovered.

   Prior to the Accelerated Cost Recovery System (ACRS), most capital purchases were depreciated using a straight line technique, that allowed for the depreciation of the asset over its useful life.

   a. Categorical grants
   b. BMC Software, Inc.
   c. Modified Accelerated Cost Recovery System
   d. 3M Company

7. There are several methods for calculating depreciation, generally based on either the passage of time or the level of activity (or use) of the asset.

Chapter 12. Income Taxes, Unusual Income Items, and Investments in Stocks

_____ is the simplest and most often used technique, in which the company estimates the salvage value of the asset at the end of the period during which it will be used to generate revenues (useful life), and will expense a portion of original cost in equal increments over that period.

- a. Pro forma
- b. Straight-line depreciation
- c. Closing entries
- d. Current asset

8. _____ is a term used in accounting, economics and finance to spread the cost of an asset over the span of several years.

In simple words we can say that _____ is the reduction in the value of an asset due to usage, passage of time, wear and tear, technological outdating or obsolescence, depletion, inadequacy, rot, rust, decay or other such factors.

In accounting, _____ is a term used to describe any method of attributing the historical or purchase cost of an asset across its useful life, roughly corresponding to normal wear and tear.

- a. General ledger
- b. Current asset
- c. Depreciation
- d. Net profit

9. _____ is the total cost involved in operating all production facilities of a manufacturing business. It generally applies to indirect labor and indirect cost, it also includes all costs involved in manufacturing with the exception of the cost of raw materials and direct labor. _____ also includes certain costs such as quality assurance costs, cleanup costs, and property insurance premiums.

- a. Cost driver
- b. Profit center
- c. Contribution margin analysis
- d. Factory overhead

10. In business, _____, Overhead cost or _____ expense refers to an ongoing expense of operating a business. The term _____ is usually used to group expenses that are necessary to the continued functioning of the business, but do not directly generate profits.

_____ expenses are all costs on the income statement except for direct labor and direct materials.

- a. ABC Television Network
- b. AIG
- c. Overhead
- d. Intangible assets

11. _____ is a company's financial statement that indicates how the revenue is transformed into the net income The purpose of the _____ is to show managers and investors whether the company made or lost money during the period being reported.

The important thing to remember about an _____ is that it represents a period of time.

Chapter 12. Income Taxes, Unusual Income Items, and Investments in Stocks

a. AMEX
b. AIG
c. ABC Television Network
d. Income statement

12. _____ is the corporate management term for the act of partially dismantling or otherwise reorganizing a company for the purpose of making it more profitable. Also known as corporate _____, debt _____ and financial _____.

_____ is often done as part of a bankruptcy or of a strategic takeover by another firm, such as a leveraged buyout by a private equity firm.

a. Restructuring
b. Securitization
c. Treasury company
d. Cross-border leasing

13. _____, also known as property, plant, and equipment (PP&E), is a term used in accountancy for assets and property which cannot easily be converted into cash. This can be compared with current assets such as cash or bank accounts, which are described as liquid assets. In most cases, only tangible assets are referred to as fixed.

a. Fixed asset
b. Certified Practising Accountant
c. Lower of Cost or Market
d. Remittance advice

14. In business and accounting, _____ are everything of value that is owned by a person or company. It is a claim on the property your income of a borrower. The balance sheet of a firm records the monetary value of the _____ owned by the firm.

a. Earnings before interest, taxes, depreciation and amortization
b. Accounts receivable
c. Assets
d. Accrual basis accounting

15. _____ is a term used with respect to a retailed product, indicating that the product is in the end of its product lifetime and a vendor will no longer be marketing, selling, or promoting a particular product and may also be limiting or ending support for the product. In the specific case of product sales, the term end-of-sale (EOS) has also been used. The term lifetime, after the last production date, depends on the product and is related to a customer's expected product lifetime.

a. AIG
b. ABC Television Network
c. AMEX
d. End-of-life

16. Just in Time could refer to the following:

- _____, an inventory strategy that reduces in-process inventory
- _____ compilation, a technique for improving the performance of bytecode-compiled programming systems

a. Department of the Treasury
b. Price-to-sales ratio
c. Just-in-time
d. Trailing

17. _____ is a specific term used in companies' financial reporting from the company-whole point of view. Because that use excludes the effects of changing ownership interest, an economic measure of _____ is necessary for financial analysis from the shareholders' point of view

Chapter 12. Income Taxes, Unusual Income Items, and Investments in Stocks

_____ is defined by the Financial Accounting Standards Board, or FASB, as 'the change in equity [net assets] of a business enterprise during a period from transactions and other events and circumstances from nonowner sources. It includes all changes in equity during a period except those resulting from investments by owners and distributions to owners.'

_____ is the sum of net income and other items that must bypass the income statement because they have not been realized, including items like an unrealized holding gain or loss from available for sale securities and foreign currency translation gains or losses.

a. 3M Company
b. BNSF Railway
c. BMC Software, Inc.
d. Comprehensive income

18. _____ are the earnings returned on the initial investment amount.

In the US, the Financial Accounting Standards Board (FASB) requires companies' income statements to report _____ for each of the major categories of the income statement: continuing operations, discontinued operations, extraordinary items, and net income.

The _____ formula does not include preferred dividends for categories outside of continued operations and net income.

a. Average accounting return
b. Earnings yield
c. Invested capital
d. Earnings per share

19. _____ is a subsection in equity where 'other comprehensive income' is accumulated (summed or 'aggregated'.)

The balance of _____ is presented in the Equity section of the Balance Sheet as is the Retained Earnings balance, which aggregates past and current Earnings, and past and current Dividends.

Other comprehensive income is the difference between net income and comprehensive income and represents the certain gains and losses of the enterprise.

a. Accumulated other comprehensive income
b. Operating budget
c. Authorised capital
d. Inventory turnover ratio

20. _____ is a company's earnings per share (EPS) calculated using fully diluted shares outstanding. _____ indicates a 'worst case' scenario, one in which everyone who could have received stock without purchasing it directly for the full market value did so.

To find _____, basic EPS is calculated for each of the categories on the income statement first. Then each of the dilutive securities are ranked based on their effects, from most dilutive to least dilutive and antidilutive. Then the basic EPS number is diluted one by one by applying each one, skipping any instruments that have an antidilutive effect.

a. Return on assets Du Pont
b. Return on equity
c. Diluted earnings per share
d. Yield Gap

21. _____ is a form of corporation equity ownership represented in the securities. It is a stock whose dividends are based on market fluctuations. It is dangerous in comparison to preferred shares and some other investment options, in that in the event of bankruptcy, _____ investors receive their funds after preferred stock holders, bondholders, creditors, etc. On the other hand, common shares on average perform better than preferred shares or bonds over time.
a. Growth investing
b. Common stock
c. 3M Company
d. Stock split

22. The term '_____' refers to the concept of collecting information and attempting to spot a pattern in the information. In some fields of study, the term '_____' has more formally-defined meanings.

In project management _____ is a mathematical technique that uses historical results to predict future outcome.

a. 3M Company
b. Multicollinearity
c. Regression analysis
d. Trend analysis

23. _____ are securities that can be easily converted into cash. Such securities will generally have highly liquid markets allowing the security to be sold at a reasonable price very quickly. This is a usual feature in real estate .
a. BMC Software, Inc.
b. Marketable
c. Tracking stock
d. 3M Company

24. _____ refers to the methods, practices and operations conducted to promote and sustain certain categories of commercial activity. The term is understood to have different specific meanings depending on the context. Merchandise is a sale goods at a store

In marketing, one of the definitions of _____ is the practice in which the brand or image from one product or service is used to sell another.

a. BMC Software, Inc.
b. 3M Company
c. Merchandising
d. Merchandise

25. A _____ is a fungible, negotiable instrument representing financial value. they are broadly categorized into debt securities (such as banknotes, bonds and debentures), and equity securities; e.g., common stocks. The company or other entity issuing the _____ is called the issuer.
a. BMC Software, Inc.
b. 3M Company
c. Tracking stock
d. Security

26. In economics, the concept of the _____ refers to the decision-making time frame of a firm in which at least one factor of production is fixed. Costs which are fixed in the _____ have no impact on a firms decisions. For example a firm can raise output by increasing the amount of labour through overtime.
a. Long-run
b. 3M Company
c. BMC Software, Inc.
d. Short-run

Chapter 12. Income Taxes, Unusual Income Items, and Investments in Stocks

27. In finance, a _____ is a debt security, in which the authorized issuer owes the holders a debt and, depending on the terms of the _____, is obliged to pay interest (the coupon) and/or to repay the principal at a later date, termed maturity. It is a formal contract to repay borrowed money with interest at fixed intervals.

Thus a _____ is like a loan: the issuer is the borrower, the _____ holder is the lender, and the coupon is the interest.

   a. Revenue bonds
   c. Bond

   b. Zero-coupon bond
   d. Coupon rate

28. _____ is generally understood in financial circles as the point at which revenue is recognized, typically through a transaction which involves the exchange of an asset, product, or service for cash or its equivalents.

This approach gives the accounting division a strictly objective basis for changing the books. For example, a homeowner may believe that his house has grown in value during a strong market, or fallen in value during a weak market, but until the house is actually sold for a specific price to a specific buyer, the change in value can only be estimated and is considered unrealized.

   a. Just-in-time
   c. Realization

   b. Merck ' Co., Inc.
   d. Factor

29. _____ are generally defined as increases (decreases) in the replacement costs of the assets held during a given period. _____ and losses accrue to the owners of assets and liabilities purely as a result of holding the assets or liabilities over time, without transforming them in any way.

For example, if a company holds bottles of wine in its inventory and that specific wine becomes more expensive on the market, the replacement cost of the wine in the inventory increases as it has become more expensive for the company to replace its current stock of wine.

   a. Money market
   c. Fair market value

   b. Net worth
   d. Holding gains

30. In financial accounting, a _____ or statement of financial position is a summary of a person's or organization's balances. Assets, liabilities and ownership equity are listed as of a specific date, such as the end of its financial year. A _____ is often described as a snapshot of a company's financial condition.

   a. 3M Company
   c. Notes to the financial statements

   b. Balance sheet
   d. Statement of retained earnings

31. _____ in accounting is the process of treating equity investments, usually 20-50%, in associate companies. The investor keeps such equities as an asset. Proportional share of associate company's net income increases the investment, and proportional payment of dividends decreases it.

   a. ABC Television Network
   c. Out-of-pocket

   b. AIG
   d. Equity method

32. In economic models, the _____ time frame assumes no fixed factors of production. Firms can enter or leave the marketplace, and the cost (and availability) of land, labor, raw materials, and capital goods can be assumed to vary. In contrast, in the short-run time frame, certain factors are assumed to be fixed, because there is not sufficient time for them to change.
   a. Short-run
   b. BMC Software, Inc.
   c. Long-run
   d. 3M Company

33. A _____ is the pinnacle activity involved in selling products or services in return for money or other compensation. It is an act of completion of a commercial activity.

A _____ is completed by the seller, the owner of the goods.

   a. Controlled Foreign Corporations
   b. Sale
   c. Procter ' Gamble
   d. Serial bonds

34. _____ are financial statements that factor the holding company's subsidiaries into its aggregated accounting figure. It is a representation of how the holding company is doing as a group. The consolidated accounts should provide a true and fair view of the financial and operating conditions of the group.
   a. Replacement cost
   b. Redemption value
   c. Consolidated financial statements
   d. Committee on Accounting Procedure

35. _____ are formal records of a business' financial activities.

In British English, including United Kingdom company law, _____ are often referred to as accounts, although the term _____ is also used, particularly by accountants.

_____ provide an overview of a business' financial condition in both short and long term.

   a. Statement of retained earnings
   b. 3M Company
   c. Notes to the financial statements
   d. Financial statements

36. A _____ is a company that owns enough voting stock in another firm to control management and operations by influencing or electing its board of directors; the second company being deemed as a subsidiary of the _____. The definition of a _____ differs from jurisdiction to jurisdiction, with the definition normally being defined by way of laws dealing with companies in that jurisdiction.

The _____-subsidiary company relationship is defined by Part 1.2, Division 6, Section 46 of the Corporations Act 2001 (Cth), which states:

Chapter 12. Income Taxes, Unusual Income Items, and Investments in Stocks

A body corporate (in this section called the first body) is a subsidiary of another body corporate if, and only if:

(a) the other body:

(i) controls the composition of the first body's board; or

(ii) is in a position to cast, or control the casting of, more than one-half of the maximum number of votes that might be cast at a general meeting of the first body; or

(iii) holds more than one-half of the issued share capital of the first body (excluding any part of that issued share capital that carries no right to participate beyond a specified amount in a distribution of either profits or capital); or

(b) the first body is a subsidiary of a subsidiary of the other body.

a. 3M Company
c. BMC Software, Inc.
b. Parent company
d. Subsidiary

37. A _____, in business matters, is an entity that is controlled by a bigger and more powerful entity. The controlled entity is called a company, corporation, or limited liability company, and the controlling entity is called its parent (or the parent company.) The reason for this distinction is that a lone company cannot be a _____ of any organization; only an entity representing a legal fiction as a separate entity can be a _____.

a. 3M Company
c. Parent company
b. BMC Software, Inc.
d. Subsidiary

38. In finance, the _____ or quick ratio or liquid ratio measures the ability of a company to use its near cash or quick assets to immediately extinguish or retire its current liabilities. Quick assets include those current assets that presumably can be quickly converted to cash at close to their book values.

$$\text{Quick (Acid Test) Ratio} = \frac{\text{Cash} + \text{Marketable Securities} + \text{Accounts Receivables}}{\text{Current Liabilities}}$$

Generally, the acid test ratio should be 1:1 or better, however this varies widely by industry.

a. Earnings per share
c. Inventory turnover
b. Acid-test
d. Invested capital

39. Transport or _____ is the movement of people and goods from one location to another. Transport is performed by various modes, such as air, rail, road, water, cable, pipeline and space. The field can be divided into infrastructure, vehicles, and operations.

a. BNSF Railway
c. 3M Company
b. BMC Software, Inc.
d. Transportation

Chapter 13. Bonds Payable and Investments in Bonds

1. In finance, a _____ is a debt security, in which the authorized issuer owes the holders a debt and, depending on the terms of the _____, is obliged to pay interest (the coupon) and/or to repay the principal at a later date, termed maturity. It is a formal contract to repay borrowed money with interest at fixed intervals.

   Thus a _____ is like a loan: the issuer is the borrower, the _____ holder is the lender, and the coupon is the interest.

   a. Bond
   b. Revenue bonds
   c. Coupon rate
   d. Zero-coupon bond

2. A _____ is a type of bond that allows the issuer of the bond to retain the privilege of redeeming the bond at some point before the bond reaches the date of maturity. In other words, on the call dates, the issuer has the right, but not the obligation, to buy back the bonds from the bond holders at the call price. Technically speaking, the bonds are not really bought and held by the issuer but cancelled immediately.

   a. Revenue bonds
   b. Callable bond
   c. Catastrophe bonds
   d. Zero-coupon

3. A _____ is defined as a certificate of agreement of loans which is given under the company's stamp and carries an undertaking that the _____ holder will get a fixed return (fixed on the basis of interest rates) and the principal amount whenever the _____ matures.

   In finance, a _____ is a long-term debt instrument used by governments and large companies to obtain funds. It is defined as 'any form of borrowing that commits a firm to pay interest and repay capital.

   a. Loan
   b. Credit rating
   c. Debt
   d. Debenture

4. _____ is a legal document issued to lenders and describes key terms such as the interest rate, maturity date, convertibility, pledge, promises, representations, covenants, and other terms of the bond offering. When the Offering Memorandum is prepared in advance of marketing a Bond, the indenture will typically be summarised in the 'Description of Notes' section.

   a. Sarbanes-Oxley Act
   b. False Claims Act
   c. Trust Indenture Act of 1939
   d. Bond indenture

5. In finance, a _____ is a type of bond that can be converted into shares of stock in the issuing company, usually at some pre-announced ratio. It is a hybrid security with debt- and equity-like features. Although it typically has a low coupon rate, the holder is compensated with the ability to convert the bond to common stock, usually at a substantial discount to the stock's market value.

   a. Municipal bond
   b. Convertible bond
   c. Premium bond
   d. Zero-coupon bond

6. An _____ is a legal contract between two parties, particularly for indentured labour or a term of apprenticeship but also for certain land transactions. The term comes from the medieval English '_____ of retainer' -- a legal contract written in duplicate on the same sheet, with the copies separated by cutting along a jagged line so that the teeth of the two parts could later be refitted to confirm authenticity. Each party to the deed would then retain a part.

a. Impracticability
b. Operating Lease
c. Employee Retirement Income Security Act
d. Indenture

7. _____ are financial bonds that mature in installments over a period of time. In effect, a $100,000, 5-year serial bond would mature in a $20,000 annuity over a 5-year interval. Bond issues consisting of a series of blocks of securities maturing in sequence, the coupon rate can be different.
  a. Joseph Ronald Banister
  b. Shrinkage
  c. Price-to-sales ratio
  d. Serial bonds

8. The United States _____ Act of 1939 (Trust indentureA), codified at 15 U.S.C. Â§ 77aaa through 15 U.S.C. Â§ 77bbbb, supplements the Securities Act of 1933 in the case of the distribution of debt securities.
  a. Consumer protection laws
  b. Chief Financial Officers Act of 1990
  c. Trust indenture
  d. Staple right

9. _____ is one of the four Ps of the marketing mix. The other three aspects are product, promotion, and place. It is also a key variable in microeconomic price allocation theory.
  a. Target costing
  b. Price discrimination
  c. Cost-plus pricing
  d. Pricing

10. In marketing a _____ is a ticket or document that can be exchanged for a financial discount or rebate when purchasing a product. Customarily, _____s are issued by manufacturers of consumer packaged goods or by retailers, to be used in retail stores as a part of sales promotions. They are often widely distributed through mail, magazines, newspapers, the Internet, and mobile devices such as cell phones.
  a. 3M Company
  b. Merchandising
  c. BMC Software, Inc.
  d. Coupon

11. The _____ of a bond is the amount of interest paid per year expressed as a percentage of the face value of the bond. It is the interest rate that a bond issuer will pay to a bondholder.

For example if you hold $10,000 nominal of a bond described as a 4.5% loan stock, you will receive $450 in interest each year (probably in two installments of $225 each.)

  a. Catastrophe bonds
  b. Zero-coupon
  c. Convertible bond
  d. Coupon rate

12. Discounting is a financial mechanism in which a debtor obtains the right to delay payments to a creditor, for a defined period of time, in exchange for a charge or fee. Essentially, the party that owes money in the present purchases the right to delay the payment until some future date. The _____, or charge, is simply the difference between the original amount owed in the present and the amount that has to be paid in the future to settle the debt.
  a. Risk aversion
  b. Risk
  c. Risk adjusted return on capital
  d. Discount

13. _____ measures the nominal future sum of money that a given sum of money is 'worth' at a specified time in the future assuming a certain interest rate rate of return; it is the present value multiplied by the accumulation function.

The value does not include corrections for inflation or other factors that affect the true value of money in the future. This is used in time value of money calculations.

- a. Future value
- b. Present value
- c. 3M Company
- d. Net present value

14. _____ is a fee paid on borrowed assets. It is the price paid for the use of borrowed money, or, money earned by deposited funds. Assets that are sometimes lent with _____ include money, shares, consumer goods through hire purchase, major assets such as aircraft, and even entire factories in finance lease arrangements. The _____ is calculated upon the value of the assets in the same manner as upon money.
- a. Insolvency
- b. AIG
- c. ABC Television Network
- d. Interest

15. A _____ is any one of a variety of different systems, institutions, procedures, social relations and infrastructures whereby persons trade, and goods and services are exchanged, forming part of the economy. It is an arrangement that allows buyers and sellers to exchange things. _____s vary in size, range, geographic scale, location, types and variety of human communities, as well as the types of goods and services traded.
- a. Market Failure
- b. Recession
- c. Nominal value
- d. Market

16. _____ is the value on a given date of a future payment or series of future payments, discounted to reflect the time value of money and other factors such as investment risk. _____ calculations are widely used in business and economics to provide a means to compare cash flows at different times on a meaningful 'like to like' basis.

The most commonly applied model of the time value of money is compound interest.

- a. Present value
- b. Future value
- c. 3M Company
- d. Net present value

17. _____ is the process of increasing, or accounting for, an amount over a period of time. Particular instances of the term include:

- _____, the allocation of a lump sum amount to different time periods, particularly for loans and other forms of finance, including related interest or other finance charges.
    - _____ schedule, a table detailing each periodic payment on a loan (typically a mortgage), as generated by an _____ calculator.
    - Negative _____, an _____ schedule where the loan amount actually increases through not paying the full interest
- Amortized analysis, analyzing the execution cost of algorithms over a sequence of operations.
- _____ of capital expenditures of certain assets under accounting rules, particularly intangible assets, in a manner analogous to depreciation.
- _____

a. Intangible
c. EBIT
b. Annuity
d. Amortization

18. A _____ assesses the credit worthiness of an individual, corporation, or even a country. It is an evaluation made by credit bureaus of a borrower's overall credit history. They are calculated from financial history and current assets and liabilities.
  a. Debt
  b. Loan to value
  c. Lender
  d. Credit rating

19. The term _____ is used in finance theory to refer to any terminating stream of fixed payments over a specified period of time. This usage is most commonly seen in academic discussions of finance, usually in connection with the valuation of the stream of payments, taking into account time value of money concepts such as interest rate and future value.

Examples of these are regular deposits to a savings account, monthly home mortgage payments and monthly insurance payments.

  a. Improvement
  b. Annuity
  c. Appropriation
  d. Intangible

20. A _____ is the transfer of wealth from one party (such as a person or company) to another. A _____ is usually made in exchange for the provision of goods, services or both, or to fulfill a legal obligation.

The simplest and oldest form of _____ is barter, the exchange of one good or service for another.

  a. 3M Company
  b. Payee
  c. Payment
  d. BMC Software, Inc.

21. There are several methods for calculating depreciation, generally based on either the passage of time or the level of activity (or use) of the asset.

_____ is the simplest and most often used technique, in which the company estimates the salvage value of the asset at the end of the period during which it will be used to generate revenues (useful life), and will expense a portion of original cost in equal increments over that period.

  a. Current asset
  b. Closing entries
  c. Pro forma
  d. Straight-line depreciation

22. An _____ is the price a borrower pays for the use of money they do not own, for instance a small company might borrow from a bank to kick start their business, and the return a lender receives for deferring the use of funds, by lending it to the borrower. _____s are normally expressed as a percentage rate over the period of one year.

_____s targets are also a vital tool of monetary policy and are used to control variables like investment, inflation, and unemployment.

Chapter 13. Bonds Payable and Investments in Bonds

a. AIG
c. AMEX
b. ABC Television Network
d. Interest rate

23. A _____ is like a lottery bond issued by the United Kingdom government's National Savings and Investments scheme. The government promises to buy back the bond, on request, for its original price.

_____s were introduced by the government in 1956, with the aim of encouraging saving and controlling inflation, with the first bonds going on sale on 1 November of that year.

a. Catastrophe bonds
c. Convertible bond
b. Premium Bond
d. Municipal bond

24. In economics, a _____ is a lower rated, potentially higher paying bond.

- High-yield debt

A high-risk, non-investment-grade bond with a low credit rating, usually BB or lower; as a consequence, it usually has a high yield. opposite of investment-grade bond. This content can be found on the following page:

a. BNSF Railway
c. BMC Software, Inc.
b. 3M Company
d. Junk bond

25. The term '_____' refers to the concept of collecting information and attempting to spot a pattern in the information. In some fields of study, the term '_____' has more formally-defined meanings.

In project management _____ is a mathematical technique that uses historical results to predict future outcome.

a. Trend analysis
c. Multicollinearity
b. Regression analysis
d. 3M Company

26. A _____ bond is a bond bought at a price lower than its face value, with the face value repaid at the time of maturity. It does not make periodic interest payments, or have so-called 'coupons,' hence the term _____ bond. Investors earn return from the compounded interest all paid at maturity plus the difference between the discounted price of the bond and its par value.

a. Revenue bonds
c. Catastrophe bonds
b. Callable bond
d. Zero-coupon

27. A _____ is a bond bought at a price lower than its face value, with the face value repaid at the time of maturity. It does not make periodic interest payments, or so-called 'coupons,' hence the term _____. Investors earn return from the compounded interest all paid at maturity plus the difference between the discounted price of the bond and its par value.

a. Revenue bonds
c. Municipal bond
b. Catastrophe bonds
d. Zero-coupon Bond

28. A _____ is a fund established by a government agency or business for the purpose of reducing debt.

The _____ was first used in Great Britain in the 18th century to reduce national debt. While used by Robert Walpole in 1716 and effectively in the 1720s and early 1730s, it originated in the commercial tax syndicates of the Italian peninsula of the 14th century to retire redeemable public debt of those cities.

    a. Cross-border leasing
    b. Creditor
    c. Money market
    d. Sinking fund

29. _____ is the total cost involved in operating all production facilities of a manufacturing business. It generally applies to indirect labor and indirect cost, it also includes all costs involved in manufacturing with the exception of the cost of raw materials and direct labor. _____ also includes certain costs such as quality assurance costs, cleanup costs, and property insurance premiums.

    a. Cost driver
    b. Profit center
    c. Contribution margin analysis
    d. Factory overhead

30. In business, _____, Overhead cost or _____ expense refers to an ongoing expense of operating a business. The term _____ is usually used to group expenses that are necessary to the continued functioning of the business, but do not directly generate profits.

_____ expenses are all costs on the income statement except for direct labor and direct materials.

    a. Overhead
    b. Intangible assets
    c. AIG
    d. ABC Television Network

31. _____ is often a small amount of discretionary funds in the form of cash used for expenditures where it is not sensible to make the disbursement by check, because of the inconvenience and costs of writing, signing and then cashing the check.

The most common way of accounting expenditures is to use the imprest system. The initial fund would be created by issuing a check for the desired amount.

    a. Fixed asset
    b. Minority interest
    c. Remittance advice
    d. Petty cash

32. A _____ is the pinnacle activity involved in selling products or services in return for money or other compensation. It is an act of completion of a commercial activity.

A _____ is completed by the seller, the owner of the goods.

    a. Serial bonds
    b. Procter ' Gamble
    c. Controlled Foreign Corporations
    d. Sale

33. In financial accounting, a _____ or statement of financial position is a summary of a person's or organization's balances. Assets, liabilities and ownership equity are listed as of a specific date, such as the end of its financial year. A _____ is often described as a snapshot of a company's financial condition.

a. Notes to the financial statements
b. 3M Company
c. Statement of retained earnings
d. Balance sheet

34. A _____ is a fungible, negotiable instrument representing financial value. they are broadly categorized into debt securities (such as banknotes, bonds and debentures), and equity securities; e.g., common stocks. The company or other entity issuing the _____ is called the issuer.
   a. BMC Software, Inc.
   b. 3M Company
   c. Tracking stock
   d. Security

Chapter 14. Statement of Cash Flows

1. _____ is the balance of the amounts of cash being received and paid by a business during a defined period of time, sometimes tied to a specific project. Measurement of _____ can be used

- to evaluate the state or performance of a business or project.
- to determine problems with liquidity. Being profitable does not necessarily mean being liquid. A company can fail because of a shortage of cash, even while profitable.
- to project rate of returns. The time of _____s into and out of projects are used as inputs to financial models such as internal rate of return, and net present value.
- to examine income or growth of a business when it is believed that accrual accounting concepts do not represent economic realities. Alternately, _____ can be used to 'validate' the net income generated by accrual accounting.

_____ as a generic term may be used differently depending on context, and certain _____ definitions may be adapted by analysts and users for their own uses. Common terms include operating _____ and free _____.

a. Gross income
b. Gross profit
c. Cash flow
d. Flow-through entity

2. In financial accounting, a _____ or Statement of cash flows is a financial statement that shows a company's flow of cash. The money coming into the business is called cash inflow, and money going out from the business is called cash outflow. The statement shows how changes in balance sheet and income accounts affect cash and cash equivalents, and breaks the analysis down to operating, investing, and financing activities.

a. 3M Company
b. BNSF Railway
c. Cash flow statement
d. BMC Software, Inc.

3. Just in Time could refer to the following:

- _____, an inventory strategy that reduces in-process inventory
- _____ compilation, a technique for improving the performance of bytecode-compiled programming systems

a. Trailing
b. Price-to-sales ratio
c. Just-in-time
d. Department of the Treasury

4. The term '_____' refers to the concept of collecting information and attempting to spot a pattern in the information. In some fields of study, the term '_____' has more formally-defined meanings.

In project management _____ is a mathematical technique that uses historical results to predict future outcome.

a. Regression analysis
b. Multicollinearity
c. 3M Company
d. Trend analysis

5. _____ is a specific term used in companies' financial reporting from the company-whole point of view. Because that use excludes the effects of changing ownership interest, an economic measure of _____ is necessary for financial analysis from the shareholders' point of view

_____ is defined by the Financial Accounting Standards Board, or FASB, as 'the change in equity [net assets] of a business enterprise during a period from transactions and other events and circumstances from nonowner sources. It includes all changes in equity during a period except those resulting from investments by owners and distributions to owners.'

_____ is the sum of net income and other items that must bypass the income statement because they have not been realized, including items like an unrealized holding gain or loss from available for sale securities and foreign currency translation gains or losses.

    a. BMC Software, Inc.   b. 3M Company
    c. BNSF Railway   d. Comprehensive income

6. In financial accounting, a _____ or statement of financial position is a summary of a person's or organization's balances. Assets, liabilities and ownership equity are listed as of a specific date, such as the end of its financial year. A _____ is often described as a snapshot of a company's financial condition.

    a. 3M Company   b. Statement of retained earnings
    c. Balance sheet   d. Notes to the financial statements

7. _____ is a term used in accounting, economics and finance to spread the cost of an asset over the span of several years.

In simple words we can say that _____ is the reduction in the value of an asset due to usage, passage of time, wear and tear, technological outdating or obsolescence, depletion, inadequacy, rot, rust, decay or other such factors.

In accounting, _____ is a term used to describe any method of attributing the historical or purchase cost of an asset across its useful life, roughly corresponding to normal wear and tear.

    a. Net profit   b. General ledger
    c. Current asset   d. Depreciation

8. _____ is equal to the income that a firm has after subtracting costs and expenses from the total revenue. _____ can be distributed among holders of common stock as a dividend or held by the firm as retained earnings.

The items deducted will typically include tax expense, financing expense (interest expense), and minority interest. Likewise, preferred stock dividends will be subtracted too, though they are not an expense.

    a. Net income   b. Matching principle
    c. Long-term liabilities   d. Generally accepted accounting principles

9. In business and accounting, _____ are everything of value that is owned by a person or company. It is a claim on the property your income of a borrower. The balance sheet of a firm records the monetary value of the _____ owned by the firm.

Chapter 14. Statement of Cash Flows

a. Assets

c. Accrual basis accounting

b. Accounts receivable

d. Earnings before interest, taxes, depreciation and amortization

10. _____ is the term used to refer to the standard framework of guidelines for financial accounting used in any given jurisdiction. _____ includes the standards, conventions, and rules accountants follow in recording and summarizing transactions, and in the preparation of financial statements.

Financial accounting information must be assembled and reported objectively.

a. Generally accepted accounting principles
c. General ledger

b. Current asset
d. Long-term liabilities

11. In financial accounting, a _____ is defined as an obligation of an entity arising from past transactions or events, the settlement of which may result in the transfer or use of assets, provision of services or other yielding of economic benefits in the future.

a. Resource Conservation and Recovery Act
c. Pre-emption right

b. Trust Indenture Act of 1939
d. Liability

12. A _____ is the pinnacle activity involved in selling products or services in return for money or other compensation. It is an act of completion of a commercial activity.

A _____ is completed by the seller, the owner of the goods.

a. Sale
c. Serial bonds

b. Controlled Foreign Corporations
d. Procter ' Gamble

13. _____ is a form of corporation equity ownership represented in the securities. It is a stock whose dividends are based on market fluctuations. It is dangerous in comparison to preferred shares and some other investment options, in that in the event of bankruptcy, _____ investors receive their funds after preferred stock holders, bondholders, creditors, etc. On the other hand, common shares on average perform better than preferred shares or bonds over time.

a. 3M Company
c. Growth investing

b. Stock split
d. Common stock

14. _____ are payments made by a corporation to its shareholder members. It is the portion of corporate profits paid out to stockholders. When a corporation earns a profit or surplus, that money can be put to two uses: it can either be re-invested in the business (called retained earnings), or it can be paid to the shareholders as a dividend.

a. Franking credit
c. Dividend payout ratio

b. Dividend stripping
d. Dividends

15. A _____ is the transfer of wealth from one party (such as a person or company) to another. A _____ is usually made in exchange for the provision of goods, services or both, or to fulfill a legal obligation.

The simplest and oldest form of _____ is barter, the exchange of one good or service for another.

a. 3M Company
b. Payee
c. BMC Software, Inc.
d. Payment

16. In finance, a _____ is a debt security, in which the authorized issuer owes the holders a debt and, depending on the terms of the _____, is obliged to pay interest (the coupon) and/or to repay the principal at a later date, termed maturity. It is a formal contract to repay borrowed money with interest at fixed intervals.

Thus a _____ is like a loan: the issuer is the borrower, the _____ holder is the lender, and the coupon is the interest.

a. Revenue bonds
b. Zero-coupon bond
c. Coupon rate
d. Bond

17. A _____, also client, buyer or purchaser is the buyer or user of the paid products of an individual or organization, mostly called the supplier or seller. This is typically through purchasing or renting goods or services.

a. Customer
b. BMC Software, Inc.
c. BNSF Railway
d. 3M Company

18. _____ is a company's financial statement that indicates how the revenue is transformed into the net income The purpose of the _____ is to show managers and investors whether the company made or lost money during the period being reported.

The important thing to remember about an _____ is that it represents a period of time.

a. AIG
b. ABC Television Network
c. AMEX
d. Income statement

19. In accounting, _____ has a very specific meaning. It is an outflow of cash or other valuable assets from a person or company to another person or company. This outflow of cash is generally one side of a trade for products or services that have equal or better current or future value to the buyer than to the seller.

a. AIG
b. ABC Television Network
c. AMEX
d. Expense

20. An _____, operating expenditure, operational expense, operational expenditure or OPEX is an on-going cost for running a product, business, or system. Its counterpart, a capital expenditure (CAPEX), is the cost of developing or providing non-consumable parts for the product or system. For example, the purchase of a photocopier is the CAPEX, and the annual paper and toner cost is the OPEX.

a. Operating expense
b. ABC Television Network
c. AIG
d. AMEX

21. An _____ is a tax levied on the financial income of people, corporations, or other legal entities. Various _____ systems exist, with varying degrees of tax incidence. Income taxation can be progressive, proportional, or regressive.

a. Individual Retirement Arrangement
b. Ordinary income
c. Implied level of government service
d. Income tax

Chapter 14. Statement of Cash Flows

22. _____ is a fee paid on borrowed assets. It is the price paid for the use of borrowed money, or, money earned by deposited funds. Assets that are sometimes lent with _____ include money, shares, consumer goods through hire purchase, major assets such as aircraft, and even entire factories in finance lease arrangements. The _____ is calculated upon the value of the assets in the same manner as upon money.
   a. AIG
   b. ABC Television Network
   c. Insolvency
   d. Interest

23. In finance, _____ is the interest that has accumulated since the principal investment, or since the previous interest payment if there has been one already. For a financial instrument such as a bond, interest is calculated and paid in set intervals.

The primary formula for calculating the interest accrued in a given period is:

$$I_A = T \times P \times R$$

where I_A is the _____, T is the fraction of the year, P is the principal, and R is the annualized interest rate.

   a. Accrued interest
   b. Interest
   c. AIG
   d. ABC Television Network

24. _____ relates to the cost of borrowing money. It is the price that a lender charges a borrower for the use of the lender's money. _____ is different from OPEX and CAPEX, for it relates to the capital structure of a company.
   a. Interest Expense
   b. AIG
   c. ABC Television Network
   d. Interest

25. In a company, _____ is the sum of all financial records of salaries, wages, bonuses and deductions.

A paycheck, is traditionally a paper document issued by an employer to pay an employee for services rendered. While most commonly used in the United States, recently the physical paycheck has been increasingly replaced by electronic direct deposit to bank accounts.

   a. 3M Company
   b. Tax expense
   c. Total Expense Ratio
   d. Payroll

26. In corporate finance, _____ is a cash flow available for distribution among all the security holders of a company. They include equity holders, debt holders, preferred stock holders, convertible security holders, and so on.
   a. Free cash flow
   b. Product life cycle
   c. Safety stock
   d. Pre-determined overhead rate

27. A _____ is a computer application that simulates a paper worksheet. It displays multiple cells that together make up a grid consisting of rows and columns, each cell containing either alphanumeric text or numeric values. A _____ cell may alternatively contain a formula that defines how the contents of that cell is to be calculated from the contents of any other cell (or combination of cells) each time any cell is updated.

a. Linear regression
b. Spreadsheet
c. Mutual fund
d. Merck ' Co., Inc.

Chapter 15. Financial Statement Analysis

1. _____ is one of financial audit skill which help an auditor understand the client's business and changes in the business, to identify potential risk areas and to plan other audit procedures.

_____ include comparison of financial information (data in financial statement) with

1. prior periods
2. budgets
3. forecasts
4. similar industries and so on.

It also includes consideration of predictable relationships, such as:

1. gross profit to sales,
2. payroll costs to employees,
3. financial information and non-financial information, for examples the CEO's reports and the industry news.

possible sources of information about the client include:

1. interim financial information
2. Budgets
3. Management accounts
4. Non-Financial information
5. Bank and cash records
6. VAT returns
7. Board minutes
8. Discussion or correspondance with the client at they year-end

a. Assurance service
b. External auditor
c. Analytical procedures
d. International Federation of Audit Bureaux of Circulations

2. _____ is one of a series of accounting transactions dealing with the billing of customers who owe money to a person, company or organization for goods and services that have been provided to the customer. In most business entities this is typically done by generating an invoice and mailing or electronically delivering it to the customer, who in turn must pay it within an established timeframe called credit or payment terms.

An example of a common payment term is Net 30, meaning payment is due in the amount of the invoice 30 days from the date of invoice.

a. Adjusting entries
b. Accrual
c. Accrued revenue
d. Accounts receivable

3. In financial accounting, a _____ or statement of financial position is a summary of a person's or organization's balances. Assets, liabilities and ownership equity are listed as of a specific date, such as the end of its financial year. A _____ is often described as a snapshot of a company's financial condition.

Chapter 15. Financial Statement Analysis

a. Statement of retained earnings
b. Notes to the financial statements
c. 3M Company
d. Balance sheet

4. In economics, business, retail, and accounting, a _____ is the value of money that has been used up to produce something, and hence is not available for use anymore. In economics, a _____ is an alternative that is given up as a result of a decision. In business, the _____ may be one of acquisition, in which case the amount of money expended to acquire it is counted as _____.

   a. Prime cost
   b. Cost
   c. Cost allocation
   d. Cost of quality

5. In financial accounting, _____ or cost of sales includes the direct costs attributable to the production of the goods sold by a company. This amount includes the materials cost used in creating the goods along with the direct labor costs used to produce the good. It excludes indirect expenses such as distribution costs and sales force costs.

   a. Reorder point
   b. 3M Company
   c. Cost of goods sold
   d. Finished good

6. In accounting, a _____ is an asset on the balance sheet which is expected to be sold or otherwise used up in the near future, usually within one year, or one business cycle - whichever is longer. Typical _____s include cash, cash equivalents, accounts receivable, inventory, the portion of prepaid accounts which will be used within a year, and short-term investments.

On the balance sheet, assets will typically be classified into _____s and long-term assets.

   a. Pro forma
   b. General ledger
   c. Deferred
   d. Current asset

7. In business and accounting, _____ are everything of value that is owned by a person or company. It is a claim on the property your income of a borrower. The balance sheet of a firm records the monetary value of the _____ owned by the firm.

   a. Accrual basis accounting
   b. Accounts receivable
   c. Assets
   d. Earnings before interest, taxes, depreciation and amortization

8. _____ is a company's financial statement that indicates how the revenue is transformed into the net income The purpose of the _____ is to show managers and investors whether the company made or lost money during the period being reported.

The important thing to remember about an _____ is that it represents a period of time.

   a. Income statement
   b. AMEX
   c. ABC Television Network
   d. AIG

9. _____ is a specific term used in companies' financial reporting from the company-whole point of view. Because that use excludes the effects of changing ownership interest, an economic measure of _____ is necessary for financial analysis from the shareholders' point of view

Chapter 15. Financial Statement Analysis

_____ is defined by the Financial Accounting Standards Board, or FASB, as 'the change in equity [net assets] of a business enterprise during a period from transactions and other events and circumstances from nonowner sources. It includes all changes in equity during a period except those resulting from investments by owners and distributions to owners.'

_____ is the sum of net income and other items that must bypass the income statement because they have not been realized, including items like an unrealized holding gain or loss from available for sale securities and foreign currency translation gains or losses.

    a. BNSF Railway   b. BMC Software, Inc.
    c. 3M Company   d. Comprehensive income

10. In finance, or business _____ is the ability of an entity to pay its debts with available cash. _____ can also be described as the ability of a corporation to meet its long-term fixed expenses and to accomplish long-term expansion and growth. The better a company's _____, the better it is financially.

    a. Capital asset   b. 3M Company
    c. BMC Software, Inc.   d. Solvency

11. In economics, _____ or _____ goods or real _____ refers to factors of production used to create goods or services that are not themselves significantly consumed (though they may depreciate) in the production process. _____ goods may be acquired with money or financial _____. In finance and accounting, _____ generally refers to financial wealth, especially that used to start or maintain a business.

    a. Sale   b. Consumption
    c. Debt-to-GDP ratios   d. Capital

12. The _____ is a financial ratio that measures whether or not a firm has enough resources to pay its debts over the next 12 months. It compares a firm's current assets to its current liabilities. It is expressed as follows:

$$\text{Current ratio} = \frac{\text{Current Assets}}{\text{Current Liabilities}}$$

For example, if WXY Company's current assets are $50,000,000 and its current liabilities are $40,000,000, then its _____ would be $50,000,000 divided by $40,000,000, which equals 1.25.

    a. Net Interest Income   b. Return on assets
    c. Current ratio   d. Total revenue share

13. _____ is a financial metric which represents operating liquidity available to a business. Along with fixed assets such as plant and equipment, _____ is considered a part of operating capital. It is calculated as current assets minus current liabilities.

    a. Working capital management   b. Working capital
    c. 3M Company   d. BMC Software, Inc.

Chapter 15. Financial Statement Analysis

14. In finance, the _____ or quick ratio or liquid ratio measures the ability of a company to use its near cash or quick assets to immediately extinguish or retire its current liabilities. Quick assets include those current assets that presumably can be quickly converted to cash at close to their book values.

$$\text{Quick (Acid Test) Ratio} = \frac{\text{Cash} + \text{Marketable Securities} + \text{Accounts Receivables}}{\text{Current Liabilities}}$$

Generally, the acid test ratio should be 1:1 or better, however this varies widely by industry.

a. Acid-test
b. Invested capital
c. Inventory turnover
d. Earnings per share

15. A _____ is the pinnacle activity involved in selling products or services in return for money or other compensation. It is an act of completion of a commercial activity.

A _____ is completed by the seller, the owner of the goods.

a. Procter ' Gamble
b. Sale
c. Controlled Foreign Corporations
d. Serial bonds

16. A _____, in business matters, is an entity that is controlled by a bigger and more powerful entity. The controlled entity is called a company, corporation, or limited liability company, and the controlling entity is called its parent (or the parent company.) The reason for this distinction is that a lone company cannot be a _____ of any organization; only an entity representing a legal fiction as a separate entity can be a _____.

a. BMC Software, Inc.
b. Parent company
c. Subsidiary
d. 3M Company

17. The _____ is a subset of the general ledger used in accounting. The _____ shows detail for part of the accounting records such as property and equipment, prepaid expenses, etc. The detail would include such items as date the item was purchased or expense incurred, a description of the item, the original balance, and the net book value.

a. Minority interest
b. Credit memo
c. Subledger
d. Remittance advice

18. _____ is the process of understanding the stock/product mix combined with the knowledge of the demand for stock/product.

a. AIG
b. ABC Television Network
c. AMEX
d. Inventory analysis

19. The _____ is an equation that equals the cost of goods sold divided by the average inventory. Average inventory equals beginning inventory plus ending inventory divided by 2.

The formula for _____:

$$\text{Inventory Turnover} = \frac{\text{Cost of Goods Sold}}{\text{Average Inventory}}$$

The formula for average inventory:

$$\text{Average Inventory} = \frac{\text{Beginning inventory} + \text{Ending inventory}}{2}$$

A low turnover rate may point to overstocking, obsolescence, or deficiencies in the product line or marketing effort.

- a. Upside potential ratio
- b. Inventory turnover
- c. Earnings per share
- d. Enterprise Value/Sales

20. _____, also known as property, plant, and equipment (PP&E), is a term used in accountancy for assets and property which cannot easily be converted into cash. This can be compared with current assets such as cash or bank accounts, which are described as liquid assets. In most cases, only tangible assets are referred to as fixed.
- a. Fixed asset
- b. Remittance advice
- c. Lower of Cost or Market
- d. Certified Practising Accountant

21. In financial accounting, a _____ is defined as an obligation of an entity arising from past transactions or events, the settlement of which may result in the transfer or use of assets, provision of services or other yielding of economic benefits in the future.
- a. Pre-emption right
- b. Trust Indenture Act of 1939
- c. Resource Conservation and Recovery Act
- d. Liability

22. In economic models, the _____ time frame assumes no fixed factors of production. Firms can enter or leave the marketplace, and the cost (and availability) of land, labor, raw materials, and capital goods can be assumed to vary. In contrast, in the short-run time frame, certain factors are assumed to be fixed, because there is not sufficient time for them to change.
- a. 3M Company
- b. Short-run
- c. Long-run
- d. BMC Software, Inc.

23. _____ are liabilities with a future benefit over one year, such as notes payable that mature greater than one year.

In accounting, the _____ are shown on the right wing of the balance-sheet representing the sources of funds, which are generally bounded in form of capital assets.

Examples of _____ are debentures, mortgage loans and other bank loans (note: not all bank loans are long term as not all are paid over a period greater than a year, the example is bridging loan.)

a. Long-term liabilities
b. Book value
c. Gross sales
d. Cash basis accounting

24. _____ is a fee paid on borrowed assets. It is the price paid for the use of borrowed money , or, money earned by deposited funds .Assets that are sometimes lent with _____ include money, shares, consumer goods through hire purchase, major assets such as aircraft, and even entire factories in finance lease arrangements. The _____ is calculated upon the value of the assets in the same manner as upon money.
   a. Insolvency
   b. ABC Television Network
   c. AIG
   d. Interest

25. The _____ is a financial ratio indicating the relative proportion of equity to all used to finance a company's assets. The two components are often taken from the firm's balance sheet or statement of financial position (so-called book value), but the ratio may also be calculated using market values for both, if the company's equities are publicly traded.

The _____ is especially in Central Europe a very common financial ratio while in the US the debt to _____ is more often used in financial (research) reports.

   a. Earnings yield
   b. Average accounting return
   c. Efficiency ratio
   d. Equity Ratio

26. In bookkeeping, accounting, and finance, _____ are operating revenues earned by a company when it sells its products. Revenue (_____) are reported directly on the income statement as Sales or _____.

In financial ratios that use income statement sales values, 'sales' refers to _____, not gross sales.

   a. Deferred
   b. Matching principle
   c. Historical cost
   d. Net sales

27. _____ are payments made by a corporation to its shareholder members. It is the portion of corporate profits paid out to stockholders. When a corporation earns a profit or surplus, that money can be put to two uses: it can either be re-invested in the business (called retained earnings), or it can be paid to the shareholders as a dividend.
   a. Dividend stripping
   b. Franking credit
   c. Dividend payout ratio
   d. Dividends

28. _____ is a form of corporation equity ownership represented in the securities. It is a stock whose dividends are based on market fluctuations. It is dangerous in comparison to preferred shares and some other investment options, in that in the event of bankruptcy, _____ investors receive their funds after preferred stock holders, bondholders, creditors, etc. On the other hand, common shares on average perform better than preferred shares or bonds over time.
   a. Growth investing
   b. Stock split
   c. 3M Company
   d. Common stock

29. _____ are the earnings returned on the initial investment amount.

In the US, the Financial Accounting Standards Board (FASB) requires companies' income statements to report _____ for each of the major categories of the income statement: continuing operations, discontinued operations, extraordinary items, and net income.

The _____ formula does not include preferred dividends for categories outside of continued operations and net income.

a. Earnings yield
b. Average accounting return
c. Invested capital
d. Earnings per share

30. A _____ is the dividend paid to common stock owners from the profits of the company. Like other dividends, the payout is in the form of cash or other like stock. The law may regulate the size of the _____ particularly when the payout is a cash distribution tantamount to a liquidation.

a. Due diligence
b. Types of business
c. Tax patent
d. Common stock Dividend

31. The _____ on a company stock is the company's annual dividend payments divided by its market cap, or the dividend per share divided by the price per share. It is often expressed as a percentage.

Dividend payments on preferred shares are stipulated by the prospectus.

a. Dividends
b. Dividend yield
c. Dividend payout ratio
d. Dividend stripping

32. In finance, the term _____ describes the amount in cash that returns to the owners of a security. Normally it does not include the price variations, at the difference of the total return. _____ applies to various stated rates of return on stocks (common and preferred, and convertible), fixed income instruments (bonds, notes, bills, strips, zero coupon), and some other investment type insurance products (e.g. annuities.)

a. Corporate Bond
b. Yield
c. Pension System
d. Capital

33. An _____ is a comprehensive report on a company's activities throughout the preceding year. _____s are intended to give shareholders and other interested persons information about the company's activities and financial performance. Most jurisdictions require companies to prepare and disclose _____s, and many require the _____ to be filed at the company's registry.

a. Annual report
b. AMEX
c. ABC Television Network
d. AIG

34. An _____ is a term used in behavioral economics to describe those types of behaviors that impose costs on a person in the long-run that are not taken into account when making decisions in the present. Classical Economics discourages government from creating legislation that targets internalities, because it is assumed that the consumer takes these personal costs into account when paying for the good that causes the _____. For example, cigarettes should be taxed because of the negative consumption externalities that they impose, such as second-hand smoke, not because the smoker harms him or herself by smoking.

a. Inventory turnover ratio
b. Authorised capital
c. Internality
d. Operating budget

Chapter 15. Financial Statement Analysis

35. In accounting and organizational theory, _____ is defined as a process effected by an organization's structure, work and authority flows, people and management information systems, designed to help the organization accomplish specific goals or objectives. It is a means by which an organization's resources are directed, monitored, and measured. It plays an important role in preventing and detecting fraud and protecting the organization's resources, both physical (e.g., machinery and property) and intangible (e.g., reputation or intellectual property such as trademarks.)
   - a. Auditor independence
   - b. Internal control
   - c. Audit risk
   - d. Audit committee

36. The _____ of 2002 (Pub.L. 107-204, 116 Stat. 745, enacted July 30, 2002), also known as the Public Company Accounting Reform and Investor Protection Act of 2002, is a United States federal law enacted on July 30, 2002 in response to a number of major corporate and accounting scandals including those affecting Enron, Tyco International, Adelphia, Peregrine Systems and WorldCom. The legislation establishes new or enhanced standards for all U.S. public company boards, management, and public accounting firms. It does not apply to privately held companies.
   - a. Burden of proof
   - b. Tax lien
   - c. Staple right
   - d. Sarbanes-Oxley Act

37. _____ is a style of investment strategy. Those who follow this style, known as growth investors, invest in companies that exhibit signs of above-average growth, even if the share price appears expensive in terms of metrics such as price-to-earning or price-to-book ratios. In typical usage, the term '_____' contrasts with the strategy known as value investing.
   - a. Growth investing
   - b. Stockholder
   - c. Stock split
   - d. 3M Company

38. _____ is an investment paradigm that derives from the ideas on investment and speculation that Ben Graham ' David Dodd began teaching at Columbia Business School in 1928 and subsequently developed in their 1934 text Security Analysis. Although _____ has taken many forms since its inception, it generally involves buying securities whose shares appear underpriced by some form(s) of fundamental analysis. As examples, such securities may be stock in public companies that trade at discounts to book value or tangible book value, have high dividend yields, have low price-to-earning multiples or have low price-to-book ratios.
   - a. BMC Software, Inc.
   - b. 3M Company
   - c. BNSF Railway
   - d. Value investing

Chapter 16. Managerial Accounting Concepts and Principles

1. _____ is concerned with the provisions and use of accounting information to managers within organizations, to provide them with the basis to make informed business decisions that will allow them to be better equipped in their management and control functions.

In contrast to financial accountancy information, _____ information is:

- usually confidential and used by management, instead of publicly reported;
- forward-looking, instead of historical;
- pragmatically computed using extensive management information systems and internal controls, instead of complying with accounting standards.

This is because of the different emphasis: _____ information is used within an organization, typically for decision-making.

   a. Management accounting   b. Governmental accounting
   c. Grenzplankostenrechnung   d. Nonassurance services

2. An _____ is a practitioner of accountancy, which is the measurement, disclosure or provision of assurance about financial information that helps managers, investors, tax authorities and other decision makers make resource allocation decisions.

The word '_____' is derived from the French 'Compter' which took its origin from the Latin 'Computare'. The word was formerly written in English as 'Accomptant', but in process of time the word, which was always pronounced by dropping the 'p', became gradually changed both in pronunciation and in orthography to its present form.

   a. AMEX   b. Accountant
   c. ABC Television Network   d. AIG

3. _____ is the term used to refer to the standard framework of guidelines for financial accounting used in any given jurisdiction. _____ includes the standards, conventions, and rules accountants follow in recording and summarizing transactions, and in the preparation of financial statements.

Financial accounting information must be assembled and reported objectively.

   a. Long-term liabilities   b. General ledger
   c. Generally accepted accounting principles   d. Current asset

4. _____ is a process of planning and controlling the performance or execution of any type of activity, such as:

- a project (project _____) or
- a process (process _____, sometimes referred to as the process performance measurement and management system.)

Organization's senior management is responsible for carrying out its _____.

Chapter 16. Managerial Accounting Concepts and Principles

a. BNSF Railway
c. 3M Company
b. BMC Software, Inc.
d. Management process

5. An _____, or organogram(me)) is a diagram that shows the structure of an organization and the relationships and relative ranks of its parts and positions/jobs. The term is also used for similar diagrams, for example ones showing the different elements of a field of knowledge or a group of languages. The French Encyclopédie had one of the first _____s of knowledge in general.
    a. AIG
    c. AMEX
    b. Organizational chart
    d. ABC Television Network

6. _____ is a demonstration of a process -- such as a variable, term, or object -- relative in terms of the specific process or set of validation tests used to determine its presence and quantity. Properties described in this manner must be sufficiently accessible, so that persons other than the definer may independently measure or test for them at will. An _____ is generally designed to model a conceptual definition.
    a. AMEX
    c. Operational definition
    b. AIG
    d. ABC Television Network

7. An _____ is a subset of strategic work plan. It describes short-term ways of achieving milestones and explains how, or what portion of, a strategic plan will be put into operation during a given operational period, in the case of commercial application, a fiscal year or another given budgetary term. An operational plan is the basis for, and justification of an annual operating budget request.
    a. AMEX
    c. ABC Television Network
    b. Operational planning
    d. AIG

8. _____ is an organization's process of defining its strategy and making decisions on allocating its resources to pursue this strategy, including its capital and people. Various business analysis techniques can be used in _____, including SWOT analysis (Strengths, Weaknesses, Opportunities, and Threats) and PEST analysis (Political, Economic, Social, and Technological analysis) or STEER analysis involving Socio-cultural, Technological, Economic, Ecological, and Regulatory factors and EPISTEL (Environment, Political, Informatic, Social, Technological, Economic and Legal)

_____ is the formal consideration of an organization's future course. All _____ deals with at least one of three key questions:

1. 'What do we do?'
2. 'For whom do we do it?'
3. 'How do we excel?'

In business _____, the third question is better phrased 'How can we beat or avoid competition?'. (Bradford and Duncan, page 1.)

a. 3M Company
c. BMC Software, Inc.
b. BNSF Railway
d. Strategic planning

9. _____ can be regarded as an outcome of mental processes (cognitive process) leading to the selection of a course of action among several alternatives. Every _____ process produces a final choice. The output can be an action or an opinion of choice.

a. 3M Company
c. BNSF Railway
b. Decision making
d. BMC Software, Inc.

10. _____ describes the situation when output from (or information about the result of) an event or phenomenon in the past will influence the same event/phenomenon in the present or future. When an event is part of a chain of cause-and-effect that forms a circuit or loop, then the event is said to 'feed back' into itself.

_____ is also a synonym for:

- _____ Signal; the information about the initial event that is the basis for subsequent modification of the event.
- _____ Loop; the causal path that leads from the initial generation of the _____ signal to the subsequent modification of the event.

_____ is a mechanism, process or signal that is looped back to control a system within itself. Such a loop is called a _____ loop.

a. 3M Company
c. Feedback
b. Controllable
d. BMC Software, Inc.

11. _____ is a 'policy by which management devotes its time to investigating only those situations in which actual results differ significantly from planned results. The idea is that management should spend its valuable time concentrating on the more important items (such as shaping the company's future strategic course.) Attention is given only to material deviations requiring investigation.'

It is not entirely synonymous with the concept of exception management in that it describes a policy where absolute focus is on exception management, in contrast to moderate application of exception management.

a. Management by exception
c. Best practice
b. Management by objectives
d. Cash cow

12. In economics, business, retail, and accounting, a _____ is the value of money that has been used up to produce something, and hence is not available for use anymore. In economics, a _____ is an alternative that is given up as a result of a decision. In business, the _____ may be one of acquisition, in which case the amount of money expended to acquire it is counted as _____.

a. Cost of quality
c. Cost allocation
b. Prime cost
d. Cost

13. _____ is a term that denotes the measurements used as the quantitative basis for the informed management of sustainability. The metrics used for the measurement of sustainability (involving the sustainability of environmental, social and economic domains, both individually and in various combinations) include indicators, benchmarks, audits, indexes, accounting and reporting systems and more, and they can apply on all scales from global to local.

From an environmental perspective _____ can be regarded as a quantitative aspect of resource management that compares the demand on ecosystem services with the available supply.

Chapter 16. Managerial Accounting Concepts and Principles

a. Data protection
c. Competition law
b. Chief financial officer
d. Sustainability measurement

14. Just in Time could refer to the following:

- _____, an inventory strategy that reduces in-process inventory
- _____ compilation, a technique for improving the performance of bytecode-compiled programming systems

a. Trailing
c. Price-to-sales ratio
b. Department of the Treasury
d. Just-in-time

15. _____ concern the operation of a facility, as opposed to maintenance, supply and distribution, health, and safety, emergency response, human resources, security, information technology and other infrastructural support organizations.

Personnel that make up 'operations' are

- operators
- engineers
- technicians
- management

This is mainly in a manufacturing setting.

a. Realization
c. Consolidated financial statements
b. Manufacturing Operations
d. Trade name

16. A _____ is a tangible input for a product manufactured/Service provided, like labor or material. For example a cloth manufacturing firm requires some amount of predetermined labor and predetermined raw material for any amount of cloth being manufactured. The cost of employing labor can be directly fixed as 'per man per hour' or 'per man per day', so the labor is a _____ as you can directly associate cost with it.

a. 3M Company
c. Round-tripping
b. Residual value
d. Cost object

17. _____ are costs that are not directly accountable to a particular function or product. _____ may be either fixed or variable. _____ include taxes, administration, personnel and security costs, and are also known as overhead.

a. Activity-based costing
c. ABC Television Network
b. Indirect costs
d. Activity-based management

18. _____ is the total cost involved in operating all production facilities of a manufacturing business. It generally applies to indirect labor and indirect cost, it also includes all costs involved in manufacturing with the exception of the cost of raw materials and direct labor. _____ also includes certain costs such as quality assurance costs, cleanup costs, and property insurance premiums.

a. Profit center
c. Factory overhead
b. Contribution margin analysis
d. Cost driver

Chapter 16. Managerial Accounting Concepts and Principles 119

19. Direct labor and overhead are often called conversion cost while direct material and direct labor are often referred to as _____.

For example, a manufacturing firm pays for raw materials. When activity is decreased, less raw material is used, and so the spending for raw materials falls.

a. Cost accounting
b. Marginal cost
c. Cost-volume-profit analysis
d. Prime cost

20. Project _____: The project _____ is a prediction of the costs associated with a particular company project. These costs include labor, materials, and other related expenses. The project _____ is often broken down into specific tasks, with task _____s assigned to each.

a. BNSF Railway
b. BMC Software, Inc.
c. Budget
d. 3M Company

21. In business, _____, Overhead cost or _____ expense refers to an ongoing expense of operating a business. The term _____ is usually used to group expenses that are necessary to the continued functioning of the business, but do not directly generate profits.

_____ expenses are all costs on the income statement except for direct labor and direct materials.

a. Overhead
b. Intangible assets
c. AIG
d. ABC Television Network

22. In financial accounting, a _____ or statement of financial position is a summary of a person's or organization's balances. Assets, liabilities and ownership equity are listed as of a specific date, such as the end of its financial year. A _____ is often described as a snapshot of a company's financial condition.

a. Balance sheet
b. Notes to the financial statements
c. 3M Company
d. Statement of retained earnings

23. _____ or in-process inventory includes the set at large of unfinished items for products in a production process. These items are not yet completed but either just being fabricated or waiting in a queue for further processing or in a buffer storage. The term is used in production and supply chain management.

a. BNSF Railway
b. 3M Company
c. Work in process
d. BMC Software, Inc.

24. _____ are formal records of a business' financial activities.

In British English, including United Kingdom company law, _____ are often referred to as accounts, although the term _____ is also used, particularly by accountants.

_____ provide an overview of a business' financial condition in both short and long term.

a. 3M Company
b. Notes to the financial statements
c. Statement of retained earnings
d. Financial statements

Chapter 16. Managerial Accounting Concepts and Principles

25. _____s are goods that have completed the manufacturing process but have not yet been sold or distributed to the end user.

Manufacturing has three classes of inventory:

1. Raw material
2. Work in process
3. _____s

A good purchased as a 'raw material' goes into the manufacture of a product. A good only partially completed during the manufacturing process is called 'work in process'. When the good is completed as to manufacturing but not yet sold or distributed to the end-user is called a '_____'.

a. 3M Company
c. Reorder point
b. Finished good
d. FIFO and LIFO accounting

26. _____ refers to the methods, practices and operations conducted to promote and sustain certain categories of commercial activity. The term is understood to have different specific meanings depending on the context. Merchandise is a sale goods at a store

In marketing, one of the definitions of _____ is the practice in which the brand or image from one product or service is used to sell another.

a. 3M Company
c. Merchandise
b. BMC Software, Inc.
d. Merchandising

27. In finance, a _____ is a debt security, in which the authorized issuer owes the holders a debt and, depending on the terms of the _____, is obliged to pay interest (the coupon) and/or to repay the principal at a later date, termed maturity. It is a formal contract to repay borrowed money with interest at fixed intervals.

Thus a _____ is like a loan: the issuer is the borrower, the _____ holder is the lender, and the coupon is the interest.

a. Zero-coupon bond
c. Coupon rate
b. Bond
d. Revenue bonds

28. _____ is a company's financial statement that indicates how the revenue is transformed into the net income The purpose of the _____ is to show managers and investors whether the company made or lost money during the period being reported.

The important thing to remember about an _____ is that it represents a period of time.

a. AIG
c. AMEX
b. ABC Television Network
d. Income statement

Chapter 17. Job Order Cost Systems

1. In economics, business, retail, and accounting, a _____ is the value of money that has been used up to produce something, and hence is not available for use anymore. In economics, a _____ is an alternative that is given up as a result of a decision. In business, the _____ may be one of acquisition, in which case the amount of money expended to acquire it is counted as _____.
   - a. Cost of quality
   - b. Prime cost
   - c. Cost allocation
   - d. Cost

2. In management accounting, _____ establishes budget and actual cost of operations, processes, departments or product and the analysis of variances, profitability or social use of funds. Managers use _____ to support decision-making to cut a company's costs and improve profitability. As a form of management accounting, _____ need not follow standards such as GAAP, because its primary use is for internal managers, rather than outside users, and what to compute is instead decided pragmatically.
   - a. Cost-volume-profit analysis
   - b. Prime cost
   - c. Marginal cost
   - d. Cost accounting

3. A _____ is an internal document extensively used by projects-based, manufacturing, building and fabrication businesses. A _____ may be for products and/or services. In a manufacturing environment, a _____ is used to signal the start of a manufacturing process and will most probably be linked to a bill of material.
   - a. Six Sigma
   - b. Make to order
   - c. Lean manufacturing
   - d. Job order

4. _____ are typically small manufacturing operations that handle specialized manufacturing processes such as small customer orders or small batch jobs. _____ typically move on to different jobs (possibly with different customers) when each job is completed. By nature of this type of manufacturing operation, _____ are usually specialized in skill and processes.
   - a. BNSF Railway
   - b. 3M Company
   - c. Job shops
   - d. BMC Software, Inc.

5. In financial accounting, a _____ or statement of financial position is a summary of a person's or organization's balances. Assets, liabilities and ownership equity are listed as of a specific date, such as the end of its financial year. A _____ is often described as a snapshot of a company's financial condition.
   - a. Notes to the financial statements
   - b. Statement of retained earnings
   - c. 3M Company
   - d. Balance sheet

6. An _____ or bill is a commercial document issued by a seller to the buyer, indicating the products, quantities, and agreed prices for products or services the seller has provided the buyer. An _____ indicates the buyer must pay the seller, according to the payment terms.

   In the rental industry, an _____ must include a specific reference to the duration of the time being billed, so rather than quantity, price and discount the invoicing amount is based on quantity, price, discount and duration.
   - a. Invoice
   - b. ABC Television Network
   - c. AMEX
   - d. AIG

Chapter 17. Job Order Cost Systems

7. In accounting, the _____ is an account in the general ledger to which a corresponding subsidiary ledger has been created. The subsidiary ledger allows for tracking transactions within the _____ in more detail. Individual transactions are posted both to the _____ and the corresponding subsidiary ledger, and the totals for both are compared when preparing a trial balance to ensure accuracy.
   a. Controlling account
   b. Debit
   c. Bookkeeping
   d. Debit and credit

8. _____ or in-process inventory includes the set at large of unfinished items for products in a production process. These items are not yet completed but either just being fabricated or waiting in a queue for further processing or in a buffer storage. The term is used in production and supply chain management.
   a. 3M Company
   b. BMC Software, Inc.
   c. BNSF Railway
   d. Work in process

9. Employment is a contract between two parties, one being the employer and the other being the _____. An _____ may be defined as: 'A person in the service of another under any contract of hire, express or implied, oral or written, where the employer has the power or right to control and direct the _____ in the material details of how the work is to be performed.' Black's Law Dictionary page 471 (5th ed. 1979.)
   a. AIG
   b. ABC Television Network
   c. AMEX
   d. Employee

10. _____ and benefits in kind are various non-wage compensations provided to employees in addition to their normal wages or salaries. Where an employee exchanges (cash) wages for some other form of benefit, this is generally referred to as a 'salary sacrifice' arrangement. In most countries, most kinds of _____ are taxable to at least some degree.
    a. AMEX
    b. Employee benefits
    c. ABC Television Network
    d. AIG

11. _____ is a process of attributing cost to particular cost centres. For example the wage of the driver of the purchasing department can be allocated to the purchasing department cost centre. It is not necessary to share the wage cost over several different cost centers.
    a. Cost of quality
    b. Cost allocation
    c. Variable cost
    d. Cost accounting

12. _____ is the total cost involved in operating all production facilities of a manufacturing business. It generally applies to indirect labor and indirect cost, it also includes all costs involved in manufacturing with the exception of the cost of raw materials and direct labor. _____ also includes certain costs such as quality assurance costs, cleanup costs, and property insurance premiums.
    a. Profit center
    b. Cost driver
    c. Contribution margin analysis
    d. Factory overhead

13. In business, _____, Overhead cost or _____ expense refers to an ongoing expense of operating a business. The term _____ is usually used to group expenses that are necessary to the continued functioning of the business, but do not directly generate profits.

    _____ expenses are all costs on the income statement except for direct labor and direct materials.

Chapter 17. Job Order Cost Systems

a. AIG
b. Intangible assets
c. ABC Television Network
d. Overhead

14. _____ is a costing model that identifies activities in an organization and assigns the cost of each activity resource to all products and services according to the actual consumption by each: it assigns more indirect costs (overhead) into direct costs.

In this way an organization can establish the true cost of its individual products and services for the purposes of identifying and eliminating those which are unprofitable and lowering the prices of those which are overpriced.

In a business organization, the ABC methodology assigns an organization's resource costs through activities to the products and services provided to its customers.

a. Activity-based costing
b. Activity-based management
c. Indirect costs
d. ABC Television Network

15. _____ is the process whereby companies use cost accounting to report or control the various costs of doing business.

The term _____ is widely used in business today. Unfortunately _____ has no uniform definition.

a. Factory overhead
b. Cost Management
c. Contribution margin
d. Cost driver

16. In financial accounting, _____ or cost of sales includes the direct costs attributable to the production of the goods sold by a company. This amount includes the materials cost used in creating the goods along with the direct labor costs used to produce the good. It excludes indirect expenses such as distribution costs and sales force costs.

a. Reorder point
b. Finished good
c. 3M Company
d. Cost of goods sold

17. _____s are goods that have completed the manufacturing process but have not yet been sold or distributed to the end user.

Manufacturing has three classes of inventory:

1. Raw material
2. Work in process
3. _____s

A good purchased as a 'raw material' goes into the manufacture of a product. A good only partially completed during the manufacturing process is called 'work in process'. When the good is completed as to manufacturing but not yet sold or distributed to the end-user is called a '_____'.

a. Reorder point
b. Finished good
c. FIFO and LIFO accounting
d. 3M Company

18. A _____ is the pinnacle activity involved in selling products or services in return for money or other compensation. It is an act of completion of a commercial activity.

A _____ is completed by the seller, the owner of the goods.

a. Controlled Foreign Corporations
b. Serial bonds
c. Procter ' Gamble
d. Sale

19. In accounting, _____ has a very specific meaning. It is an outflow of cash or other valuable assets from a person or company to another person or company. This outflow of cash is generally one side of a trade for products or services that have equal or better current or future value to the buyer than to the seller.
a. AIG
b. AMEX
c. ABC Television Network
d. Expense

20. _____ can be regarded as an outcome of mental processes (cognitive process) leading to the selection of a course of action among several alternatives. Every _____ process produces a final choice. The output can be an action or an opinion of choice.
a. Decision making
b. BNSF Railway
c. 3M Company
d. BMC Software, Inc.

Chapter 18. Process Cost Systems

1. _____ is an accounting methodology that traces and accumulates direct costs, and allocates indirect costs of a manufacturing process. Costs are assigned to products, usually in a large batch, which might include an entire month's production. Eventually, costs have to be allocated to individual units of product.
   a. Cost management
   b. Cost driver
   c. Process costing
   d. Contribution margin

2. In economics, business, retail, and accounting, a _____ is the value of money that has been used up to produce something, and hence is not available for use anymore. In economics, a _____ is an alternative that is given up as a result of a decision. In business, the _____ may be one of acquisition, in which case the amount of money expended to acquire it is counted as _____.
   a. Cost of quality
   b. Prime cost
   c. Cost
   d. Cost allocation

3. A _____ is an internal document extensively used by projects-based, manufacturing, building and fabrication businesses. A _____ may be for products and/or services. In a manufacturing environment, a _____ is used to signal the start of a manufacturing process and will most probably be linked to a bill of material.
   a. Job order
   b. Make to order
   c. Six Sigma
   d. Lean manufacturing

4. Under the average-cost method, it is assumed that the cost of inventory is based on the _____ of the goods available for sale during the period. _____ is computed by dividing the total cost of goods available for sale by the total units available for sale. This gives a weighted-average unit cost that is applied to the units in the ending inventory.
   a. Average cost
   b. ABC Television Network
   c. Inventory turnover ratio
   d. AIG

5. Under the _____, it is assumed that the cost of inventory is based on the average cost of the goods available for sale during the period. Average cost is computed by dividing the total cost of goods available for sale by the total units available for sale. This gives a weighted-average unit cost that is applied to the units in the ending inventory.
   a. AIG
   b. AMEX
   c. ABC Television Network
   d. Average-cost method

6. A _____ has several related meanings:

   - a daily record of events or business; a private _____ is usually referred to as a diary.
   - a newspaper or other periodical, in the literal sense of one published each day;
   - many publications issued at stated intervals, such as magazines, or scholarly academic _____s, or the record of the transactions of a society, are often called _____s. Although _____ is sometimes used, erroneously, as a synonym for 'magazine,' in academic use, a _____ refers to a serious, scholarly publication, most often peer-reviewed. A non-scholarly magazine written for an educated audience about an industry or an area of professional activity is usually called a professional magazine.

The word 'journalist' for one whose business is writing for the public press has been in use since the end of the 17th century.

Open access _____s are scholarly _____s that are available to the reader without financial or other barrier other than access to the internet itself. Some are subsidized, and some require payment on behalf of the author. Subsidized _____s are financed by an academic institution or a government information center.

a. Journal
b. 3M Company
c. BMC Software, Inc.
d. BNSF Railway

7. _____ can be regarded as an outcome of mental processes (cognitive process) leading to the selection of a course of action among several alternatives. Every _____ process produces a final choice. The output can be an action or an opinion of choice.
   a. BMC Software, Inc.
   b. BNSF Railway
   c. 3M Company
   d. Decision making

8. Just in Time could refer to the following:

   • _____, an inventory strategy that reduces in-process inventory
   • _____ compilation, a technique for improving the performance of bytecode-compiled programming systems

   a. Just-in-time
   b. Price-to-sales ratio
   c. Trailing
   d. Department of the Treasury

9. In finance, the term _____ describes the amount in cash that returns to the owners of a security. Normally it does not include the price variations, at the difference of the total return. _____ applies to various stated rates of return on stocks (common and preferred, and convertible), fixed income instruments (bonds, notes, bills, strips, zero coupon), and some other investment type insurance products (e.g. annuities.)
   a. Corporate Bond
   b. Capital
   c. Pension System
   d. Yield

Chapter 19. Cost Behavior and Cost-Volume-Profit Analysis

1. In economics, business, retail, and accounting, a _____ is the value of money that has been used up to produce something, and hence is not available for use anymore. In economics, a _____ is an alternative that is given up as a result of a decision. In business, the _____ may be one of acquisition, in which case the amount of money expended to acquire it is counted as _____.

   a. Cost of quality
   b. Cost allocation
   c. Prime cost
   d. Cost

2. _____s are expenses that change in proportion to the activity of a business. In other words, _____ is the sum of marginal costs. It can also be considered normal costs.

   a. Cost accounting
   b. Fixed costs
   c. Quality costs
   d. Variable cost

3. In economics, _____ are business expenses that are not dependent on the activities of the business They tend to be time-related, such as salaries or rents being paid per month. This is in contrast to variable costs, which are volume-related (and are paid per quantity.)

   In management accounting, _____ are defined as expenses that do not change in proportion to the activity of a business, within the relevant period or scale of production.

   a. Cost of quality
   b. Marginal cost
   c. Fixed costs
   d. Cost accounting

4. In cost-volume-profit analysis, a form of management accounting, _____ is the marginal profit per unit sale. It is a useful quantity in carrying out various calculations, and can be used as a measure of operating leverage.

   The Total _____ is Total Revenue (TR, or Sales) minus Total Variable Cost (TVC):

   Tcontribution margin = TR − TVC

   The Unit _____ (C) is Unit Revenue (Price, P) minus Unit Variable Cost (V):

   C = P − V

   The _____ Ratio is the percentage of Contribution over Total Revenue, which can be calculated from the unit contribution over unit price or total contribution over Total Revenue:

   $$\frac{C}{P} = \frac{P-V}{P} = \frac{\text{Unit Contribution Margin}}{\text{Price}} = \frac{\text{Total Contribution Margin}}{\text{Total Revenue}}$$

   For instance, if the price is $10 and the unit variable cost is $2, then the unit _____ is $8, and the _____ ratio is $8/$10 = 80%.

   a. Factory overhead
   b. Profit center
   c. Cost driver
   d. Contribution margin

Chapter 19. Cost Behavior and Cost-Volume-Profit Analysis

5. _____ is one of a series of accounting transactions dealing with the billing of customers who owe money to a person, company or organization for goods and services that have been provided to the customer. In most business entities this is typically done by generating an invoice and mailing or electronically delivering it to the customer, who in turn must pay it within an established timeframe called credit or payment terms.

An example of a common payment term is Net 30, meaning payment is due in the amount of the invoice 30 days from the date of invoice.

- a. Adjusting entries
- b. Accrual
- c. Accrued revenue
- d. Accounts receivable

6. In finance, the _____ or quick ratio or liquid ratio measures the ability of a company to use its near cash or quick assets to immediately extinguish or retire its current liabilities. Quick assets include those current assets that presumably can be quickly converted to cash at close to their book values.

$$\text{Quick (Acid Test) Ratio} = \frac{\text{Cash} + \text{Marketable Securities} + \text{Accounts Receivables}}{\text{Current Liabilities}}$$

Generally, the acid test ratio should be 1:1 or better, however this varies widely by industry.

- a. Inventory turnover
- b. Invested capital
- c. Acid-test
- d. Earnings per share

7. _____, in managerial economics is a form of cost accounting. It is a simplified model, useful for elementary instruction and for short-run decisions.

Cost-volume-profit (CVP) analysis expands the use of information provided by breakeven analysis.

- a. Cost accounting
- b. Cost of quality
- c. Fixed costs
- d. Cost-volume-profit Analysis

8. _____ is a company's financial statement that indicates how the revenue is transformed into the net income The purpose of the _____ is to show managers and investors whether the company made or lost money during the period being reported.

The important thing to remember about an _____ is that it represents a period of time.

- a. AIG
- b. Income statement
- c. ABC Television Network
- d. AMEX

9. In economics ' business, specifically cost accounting, the _____ is the point at which cost or expenses and revenue are equal: there is no net loss or gain, and one has 'broken even'. A profit or a loss has not been made, although opportunity costs have been paid, and capital has received the risk-adjusted, expected return.

Chapter 19. Cost Behavior and Cost-Volume-Profit Analysis

For example, if the business sells less than 200 tables each month, it will make a loss, if it sells more, it will be a profit.

a. Defined benefit pension plan
b. BMC Software, Inc.
c. 3M Company
d. Break-even point

10. _____ in economics and business is the result of an exchange and from that trade we assign a numerical monetary value to a good, service or asset. If Alice trades Bob 4 apples for an orange, the _____ of an orange is 4 apples. Inversely, the _____ of an apple is 1/4 oranges.

a. Price
b. Pricing
c. Transactional Net Margin Method
d. Resale price maintenance

11. The term orphan drug refers to a pharmaceutical agent that has been developed specifically to treat a rare medical condition, the condition itself being referred to as an orphan disease. The assignment of orphan status to a disease and to any drugs developed to treat it is a matter of public policy in many countries, and has resulted in medical breakthroughs that would not have otherwise been achieved due to the economics of drug research and development.

The _____ of January 1983, passed in the United States with lobbying from the National Organization for Rare Disorders, is meant to encourage pharmaceutical companies to develop drugs for diseases that have a small market: under the law, companies that develop such a drug (a drug for a disorder affecting fewer than 200,000 people in the United States) may sell it without competition for seven years, and may get clinical trial tax incentives.

a. AMEX
b. AIG
c. ABC Television Network
d. Orphan Drug Act

12. _____ is the study of how the variation (uncertainty) in the output of a mathematical model can be apportioned, qualitatively or quantitatively, to different sources of variation in the input of a model.

In more general terms uncertainty and sensitivity analyses investigate the robustness of a study when the study includes some form of mathematical modelling. While uncertainty analysis studies the overall uncertainty in the conclusions of the study, _____ tries to identify what source of uncertainty weights more on the study's conclusions.

a. Free cash flow
b. Customer satisfaction
c. Tax profit
d. Sensitivity analysis

13. A _____ is the pinnacle activity involved in selling products or services in return for money or other compensation. It is an act of completion of a commercial activity.

A _____ is completed by the seller, the owner of the goods.

Chapter 19. Cost Behavior and Cost-Volume-Profit Analysis

a. Sale
b. Procter ' Gamble
c. Controlled Foreign Corporations
d. Serial bonds

14. The _____ is a measure of how revenue growth translates into growth in operating income. It is a measure of leverage, and of how risky (volatile) a company's operating income is.

There are various measures of _____, which can be interpreted analogously to financial leverage.

a. AlphaIC
b. Upside potential ratio
c. Information ratio
d. Operating leverage

Chapter 20. Variable Costing for Management Analysis

1. Total _____ is a method of Accounting cost which entails the full cost of manufacturing or providing a service. This includes not just the costs of materials and labour, but also of all manufacturing overheads (whether e;fixede; or e;variablee;.) One of the main reasons for absorbing overheads into the cost of units is for inventory valuation purposes.

   a. AMEX
   b. AIG
   c. ABC Television Network
   d. Absorption costing

2. _____ is a company's financial statement that indicates how the revenue is transformed into the net income The purpose of the _____ is to show managers and investors whether the company made or lost money during the period being reported.

   The important thing to remember about an _____ is that it represents a period of time.

   a. Income statement
   b. ABC Television Network
   c. AMEX
   d. AIG

3. In cost-volume-profit analysis, a form of management accounting, _____ is the marginal profit per unit sale. It is a useful quantity in carrying out various calculations, and can be used as a measure of operating leverage.

   The Total _____ is Total Revenue (TR, or Sales) minus Total Variable Cost (TVC):

   Tcontribution margin = TR − TVC

   The Unit _____ (C) is Unit Revenue (Price, P) minus Unit Variable Cost (V):

   C = P − V

   The _____ Ratio is the percentage of Contribution over Total Revenue, which can be calculated from the unit contribution over unit price or total contribution over Total Revenue:

   $$\frac{C}{P} = \frac{P-V}{P} = \frac{\text{Unit Contribution Margin}}{\text{Price}} = \frac{\text{Total Contribution Margin}}{\text{Total Revenue}}$$

   For instance, if the price is $10 and the unit variable cost is $2, then the unit _____ is $8, and the _____ ratio is $8/$10 = 80%.

   a. Cost driver
   b. Contribution margin
   c. Factory overhead
   d. Profit center

4. In economics, business, retail, and accounting, a _____ is the value of money that has been used up to produce something, and hence is not available for use anymore. In economics, a _____ is an alternative that is given up as a result of a decision. In business, the _____ may be one of acquisition, in which case the amount of money expended to acquire it is counted as _____.

   a. Cost allocation
   b. Cost of quality
   c. Cost
   d. Prime cost

Chapter 20. Variable Costing for Management Analysis

5. _____ is one of the four Ps of the marketing mix. The other three aspects are product, promotion, and place. It is also a key variable in microeconomic price allocation theory.

    a. Price discrimination
    b. Target costing
    c. Cost-plus pricing
    d. Pricing

6. A _____ is any one of a variety of different systems, institutions, procedures, social relations and infrastructures whereby persons trade, and goods and services are exchanged, forming part of the economy. It is an arrangement that allows buyers and sellers to exchange things. _____s vary in size, range, geographic scale, location, types and variety of human communities, as well as the types of goods and services traded.

    a. Nominal value
    b. Market Failure
    c. Market
    d. Recession

7. A market segmentation of people or organizations sharing one or more characteristics that cause them to have similar product and/or service needs. A true _____ meets all of the following criteria: it is distinct from other segments (different segments have different needs), it is homogeneous within the segment (exhibits common needs); it responds similarly to a market stimulus, and it can be reached by a market intervention. The term is also used when consumers with identical product and/or service needs are divided up into groups so they can be charged different amounts.

    a. Business-to-consumer
    b. Market segment
    c. Customer relationship management
    d. Value chain

8. A _____ is the pinnacle activity involved in selling products or services in return for money or other compensation. It is an act of completion of a commercial activity.

A _____ is completed by the seller, the owner of the goods.

    a. Procter ' Gamble
    b. Controlled Foreign Corporations
    c. Serial bonds
    d. Sale

9. _____ is the total cost involved in operating all production facilities of a manufacturing business. It generally applies to indirect labor and indirect cost, it also includes all costs involved in manufacturing with the exception of the cost of raw materials and direct labor. _____ also includes certain costs such as quality assurance costs, cleanup costs, and property insurance premiums.

    a. Factory overhead
    b. Contribution margin analysis
    c. Profit center
    d. Cost driver

10. In business, _____, Overhead cost or _____ expense refers to an ongoing expense of operating a business. The term _____ is usually used to group expenses that are necessary to the continued functioning of the business, but do not directly generate profits.

_____ expenses are all costs on the income statement except for direct labor and direct materials.

    a. AIG
    b. ABC Television Network
    c. Intangible assets
    d. Overhead

Chapter 20. Variable Costing for Management Analysis

11. A _____ is a commercial building for storage of goods. _____s are used by manufacturers, importers, exporters, wholesalers, transport businesses, customs, etc. They are usually large plain buildings in industrial areas of cities and towns.

   a. Warehouse
   b. BNSF Railway
   c. 3M Company
   d. BMC Software, Inc.

12. _____ is a measure of operating leverage: it measures how growth in sales translates to growth in profits.

The contribution margin is computed by using a contribution income statement: a management accounting version of the income statement that has been reformatted to group together a business's fixed and variable costs.

Contribution is different to Gross Margin in that a contribution calculation seeks to separate out variable costs (included in the contribution calculation) from fixed costs (not included in the contribution calculation) on the basis of economic analysis of the nature of the expense whereas gross margin is determined using accounting standards.

   a. Cost management
   b. Contribution margin
   c. Process costing
   d. Contribution margin analysis

13. _____ in economics and business is the result of an exchange and from that trade we assign a numerical monetary value to a good, service or asset. If Alice trades Bob 4 apples for an orange, the _____ of an orange is 4 apples. Inversely, the _____ of an apple is 1/4 oranges.

   a. Price
   b. Resale price maintenance
   c. Pricing
   d. Transactional Net Margin Method

14. _____ is one of a series of accounting transactions dealing with the billing of customers who owe money to a person, company or organization for goods and services that have been provided to the customer. In most business entities this is typically done by generating an invoice and mailing or electronically delivering it to the customer, who in turn must pay it within an established timeframe called credit or payment terms.

An example of a common payment term is Net 30, meaning payment is due in the amount of the invoice 30 days from the date of invoice.

   a. Accounts receivable
   b. Accrued revenue
   c. Accrual
   d. Adjusting entries

15. In mathematics _____s are numbers or other things that get multiplied. In particular, see:

   - Factorization, the decomposition of an object into a product of other objects
   - Integer factorization, the process of breaking down a composite number into smaller non-trivial divisors
   - A coefficient
   - A divisor of a particular number, or of an element of a monoid
   - A von Neumann algebra with a trivial center

In statistics

- _____ analysis is the study of how _____s or certain variables affect variables.

In technology:

- Human _____s, a profession that focuses on how people interact with products, tools, or procedures
- 'Functionality, Application domain, Conditions, Technology, Objects and Responsibility;', In object-oriented programming

In computer science and information technology:

- Authentication _____, a piece of information used to verify a person's identity for security purposes
- _____, a Unix command for numbers factorization
- _____ (programming language), an experimental Forth-like programming language

In television:

- The O'Reilly _____, an American talk show hosted by Bill O'Reilly on Fox News.
- The Krypton _____, a British game show hosted by Gordon Burns, formally on ITV. Also had an American version.

a. Markup
b. Sale
c. Household and Dependent Care Credit
d. Factor

Chapter 21. Budgeting

1. Project _____: The project _____ is a prediction of the costs associated with a particular company project. These costs include labor, materials, and other related expenses. The project _____ is often broken down into specific tasks, with task _____s assigned to each.
   - a. Budget
   - b. BMC Software, Inc.
   - c. BNSF Railway
   - d. 3M Company

2. In financial accounting, a _____ or statement of financial position is a summary of a person's or organization's balances. Assets, liabilities and ownership equity are listed as of a specific date, such as the end of its financial year. A _____ is often described as a snapshot of a company's financial condition.
   - a. 3M Company
   - b. Balance sheet
   - c. Statement of retained earnings
   - d. Notes to the financial statements

3. In economics, business, retail, and accounting, a _____ is the value of money that has been used up to produce something, and hence is not available for use anymore. In economics, a _____ is an alternative that is given up as a result of a decision. In business, the _____ may be one of acquisition, in which case the amount of money expended to acquire it is counted as _____.
   - a. Cost of quality
   - b. Cost
   - c. Cost allocation
   - d. Prime cost

4. In financial accounting, _____ or cost of sales includes the direct costs attributable to the production of the goods sold by a company. This amount includes the materials cost used in creating the goods along with the direct labor costs used to produce the good. It excludes indirect expenses such as distribution costs and sales force costs.
   - a. Reorder point
   - b. Cost of goods sold
   - c. Finished good
   - d. 3M Company

5. _____ describes the situation when output from (or information about the result of) an event or phenomenon in the past will influence the same event/phenomenon in the present or future. When an event is part of a chain of cause-and-effect that forms a circuit or loop, then the event is said to 'feed back' into itself.

   _____ is also a synonym for:

   - _____ Signal; the information about the initial event that is the basis for subsequent modification of the event.
   - _____ Loop; the causal path that leads from the initial generation of the _____ signal to the subsequent modification of the event.

   _____ is a mechanism, process or signal that is looped back to control a system within itself. Such a loop is called a _____ loop.

   - a. 3M Company
   - b. BMC Software, Inc.
   - c. Controllable
   - d. Feedback

6. The zeroth item is the initial item of a _____ sequence (that is, a sequence which is numbered beginning from zero rather than one), such as the non-negative integers

This kind of numbering is common in array references in computer systems, so hackers, computer scientists, and computer professionals often use zeroth where others might use first, and so forth. Although there is logical reasoning for this in programming and mathematics (as explained below), it is sometimes used in other areas as well.

   a. 3M Company   b. BNSF Railway
   c. BMC Software, Inc.   d. Zero-based

7. _____ is a technique of planning and decision-making which reverses the working process of traditional budgeting. In traditional incremental budgeting, departmental managers justify only increases over the previous year budget and what has been already spent is automatically sanctioned. No reference is made to the previous level of expenditure.

   a. BMC Software, Inc.   b. Zero-based budgeting
   c. 3M Company   d. BNSF Railway

8. In business, a _____ is a product or a business unit that generates unusually high profit margins: so high that it is responsible for a large amount of a company's operating profit. This profit far exceeds the amount necessary to maintain the _____ business, and the excess is used by the business for other purposes.

A firm is said to be acting as a _____ when its earnings per share (EPS) is equal to its dividends per share (DPS), or in other words, when a firm pays out 100% of its free cash flow (FCF) to its shareholders as dividends at the end of each accounting term.

   a. Management by exception   b. Cash cow
   c. Best practice   d. Management by objectives

9. A film _____ determines how much money will be spent on the entire film project. It involves the identification and estimation of cost items for each phase of filmmaking (development, pre-production, production, post-production and distribution.)

The budget structure is normally split into 'above-the-line' (creative) and 'below-the-line' (technical) costs.

   a. 3M Company   b. BNSF Railway
   c. Production budget   d. BMC Software, Inc.

10. A _____ is the pinnacle activity involved in selling products or services in return for money or other compensation. It is an act of completion of a commercial activity.

A _____ is completed by the seller, the owner of the goods.

   a. Procter ' Gamble   b. Serial bonds
   c. Controlled Foreign Corporations   d. Sale

Chapter 21. Budgeting

11. _____ refers to a business or organization attempting to acquire goods or services to accomplish the goals of the enterprise. Though there are several organizations that attempt to set standards in the _____ process, processes can vary greatly between organizations. Typically the word e;_____e; is not used interchangeably with the word e;procuremente;, since procurement typically includes Expediting, Supplier Quality, and Traffic and Logistics (T'L) in addition to _____.

    a. Supply chain   b. Purchasing
    c. Free port   d. Consignor

12. _____ is the total cost involved in operating all production facilities of a manufacturing business. It generally applies to indirect labor and indirect cost, it also includes all costs involved in manufacturing with the exception of the cost of raw materials and direct labor. _____ also includes certain costs such as quality assurance costs, cleanup costs, and property insurance premiums.

    a. Profit center   b. Factory overhead
    c. Contribution margin analysis   d. Cost driver

13. In business, _____, Overhead cost or _____ expense refers to an ongoing expense of operating a business. The term _____ is usually used to group expenses that are necessary to the continued functioning of the business, but do not directly generate profits.

    _____ expenses are all costs on the income statement except for direct labor and direct materials.

    a. ABC Television Network   b. Intangible assets
    c. AIG   d. Overhead

14. In accounting, _____ has a very specific meaning. It is an outflow of cash or other valuable assets from a person or company to another person or company. This outflow of cash is generally one side of a trade for products or services that have equal or better current or future value to the buyer than to the seller.

    a. Expense   b. ABC Television Network
    c. AIG   d. AMEX

15. _____ is a company's financial statement that indicates how the revenue is transformed into the net income The purpose of the _____ is to show managers and investors whether the company made or lost money during the period being reported.

    The important thing to remember about an _____ is that it represents a period of time.

    a. ABC Television Network   b. Income statement
    c. AMEX   d. AIG

16. A _____ is the transfer of wealth from one party (such as a person or company) to another. A _____ is usually made in exchange for the provision of goods, services or both, or to fulfill a legal obligation.

The simplest and oldest form of _____ is barter, the exchange of one good or service for another.

a. BMC Software, Inc.
c. Payee
b. 3M Company
d. Payment

17. In economics, _____ or _____ goods or real _____ refers to factors of production used to create goods or services that are not themselves significantly consumed (though they may depreciate) in the production process. _____ goods may be acquired with money or financial _____. In finance and accounting, _____ generally refers to financial wealth, especially that used to start or maintain a business.
    a. Sale
    c. Debt-to-GDP ratios
    b. Consumption
    d. Capital

18. A _____ is an expenditure creating future benefits. A _____ is incurred when a business spends money either to buy fixed assets or to add to the value of an existing fixed asset with a useful life that extends beyond the taxable year. Capex are used by a company to acquire or upgrade physical assets such as equipment, property, or industrial buildings.
    a. Capital flight
    c. 3M Company
    b. BMC Software, Inc.
    d. Capital expenditure

Chapter 22. Performance Evaluation Using Variances from Standard Costs

1. In economics, business, retail, and accounting, a _____ is the value of money that has been used up to produce something, and hence is not available for use anymore. In economics, a _____ is an alternative that is given up as a result of a decision. In business, the _____ may be one of acquisition, in which case the amount of money expended to acquire it is counted as _____.
   a. Prime cost
   b. Cost of quality
   c. Cost allocation
   d. Cost

2. In probability theory and statistics, the _____ of a random variable, probability distribution averaging the squared distance of its possible values from the expected value (mean.) Whereas the mean is a way to describe the location of a distribution, the _____ is a way to capture its scale or degree of being spread out. The unit of _____ is the square of the unit of the original variable.
   a. Variance
   b. Statistics
   c. Monte Carlo methods
   d. Standard Deviation

3. _____ is a Japanese philosophy that focuses on continuous improvement throughout all aspects of life. When applied to the workplace, _____ activities continually improve all functions of a business, from manufacturing to management and from the CEO to the assembly line workers. By improving standardized activities and processes, _____ aims to eliminate waste .
   a. Kaizen
   b. Procurement
   c. Proprietorship
   d. Pre-determined overhead rate

4. Project _____: The project _____ is a prediction of the costs associated with a particular company project. These costs include labor, materials, and other related expenses. The project _____ is often broken down into specific tasks, with task _____s assigned to each.
   a. 3M Company
   b. BMC Software, Inc.
   c. BNSF Railway
   d. Budget

5. _____ is systematic determination of merit, worth, and significance of something or someone using criteria against a set of standards. _____ often is used to characterize and appraise subjects of interest in a wide range of human enterprises, including the arts, criminal justice, foundations and non-profit organizations, government, health care, and other human services.

Depending on the topic of interest, there are professional groups which look to the quality and rigor of the _____ process.

   a. ABC Television Network
   b. AIG
   c. AMEX
   d. Evaluation

6. Government _____ are designed to show nonfinancial aspects of government operations. For example, a government financial report might include the number of arrests, number of convictions by crime category as well as the change (i.e., increase or decrease) in crime rate. Government _____ usually provide data on environmental conditions, education and conditions of streets and roads.
   a. BNSF Railway
   b. 3M Company
   c. BMC Software, Inc.
   d. Performance reports

7. _____ in economics and business is the result of an exchange and from that trade we assign a numerical monetary value to a good, service or asset. If Alice trades Bob 4 apples for an orange, the _____ of an orange is 4 apples. Inversely, the _____ of an apple is 1/4 oranges.
   a. Pricing
   b. Transactional Net Margin Method
   c. Resale price maintenance
   d. Price

8. The materials _____ is computed as follows:

   Vmp = (Actual Unit Cost - Standard Unit Cost) * Actual Quantity Purchased

or

   Vmp = (Actual Quantity Purchased * Actual Unit Cost) - (Actual Quantity Purchased * Standard Unit Cost.)

When the Actual Materials Price is higher than the Standard Materials Price, the variance is said to be unfavorable, since the Actual price paid on materials purchased is greater than the allowed standard. The variance is said to be favorable when the Standard materials Price is higher than the Actual Materials Price, since less money was spent in purchasing the materials than the allowed standard.

   a. Consolidated financial statements
   b. Fund accounting
   c. Price Variance
   d. Liquidating dividend

9. _____ is the total cost involved in operating all production facilities of a manufacturing business. It generally applies to indirect labor and indirect cost, it also includes all costs involved in manufacturing with the exception of the cost of raw materials and direct labor. _____ also includes certain costs such as quality assurance costs, cleanup costs, and property insurance premiums.
   a. Factory overhead
   b. Profit center
   c. Contribution margin analysis
   d. Cost driver

10. In financial accounting, a _____ or statement of financial position is a summary of a person's or organization's balances. Assets, liabilities and ownership equity are listed as of a specific date, such as the end of its financial year. A _____ is often described as a snapshot of a company's financial condition.
    a. Statement of retained earnings
    b. Balance sheet
    c. 3M Company
    d. Notes to the financial statements

11. In business, _____, Overhead cost or _____ expense refers to an ongoing expense of operating a business. The term _____ is usually used to group expenses that are necessary to the continued functioning of the business, but do not directly generate profits.

    _____ expenses are all costs on the income statement except for direct labor and direct materials.

    a. AIG
    b. Intangible assets
    c. ABC Television Network
    d. Overhead

12. _____ is a company's financial statement that indicates how the revenue is transformed into the net income The purpose of the _____ is to show managers and investors whether the company made or lost money during the period being reported.

The important thing to remember about an _____ is that it represents a period of time.

a. AMEX
c. ABC Television Network

b. AIG
d. Income statement

Chapter 23. Performance Evaluation for Decentralized Operations

1. Just in Time could refer to the following:

   - _____, an inventory strategy that reduces in-process inventory
   - _____ compilation, a technique for improving the performance of bytecode-compiled programming systems

   a. Price-to-sales ratio
   b. Just-in-time
   c. Trailing
   d. Department of the Treasury

2. In economics, business, retail, and accounting, a _____ is the value of money that has been used up to produce something, and hence is not available for use anymore. In economics, a _____ is an alternative that is given up as a result of a decision. In business, the _____ may be one of acquisition, in which case the amount of money expended to acquire it is counted as _____.

   a. Cost allocation
   b. Prime cost
   c. Cost of quality
   d. Cost

3. _____s are parts of a corporation that directly add to its profit.

   A _____ manager is held accountable for both revenues, and costs (expenses), and therefore, profits. What this means in terms of managerial responsibilities is that the manager has to drive the sales revenue generating activities which leads to cash inflows and at the same time control the cost (cash outflows) causing activities.

   a. Factory overhead
   b. Profit center
   c. Process costing
   d. Contribution margin

4. In accounting, _____ has a very specific meaning. It is an outflow of cash or other valuable assets from a person or company to another person or company. This outflow of cash is generally one side of a trade for products or services that have equal or better current or future value to the buyer than to the seller.

   a. AMEX
   b. ABC Television Network
   c. Expense
   d. AIG

5. In a company, _____ is the sum of all financial records of salaries, wages, bonuses and deductions.

   A paycheck, is traditionally a paper document issued by an employer to pay an employee for services rendered. While most commonly used in the United States, recently the physical paycheck has been increasingly replaced by electronic direct deposit to bank accounts.

   a. Payroll
   b. 3M Company
   c. Total Expense Ratio
   d. Tax expense

6. _____ is a company's financial statement that indicates how the revenue is transformed into the net income The purpose of the _____ is to show managers and investors whether the company made or lost money during the period being reported.

   The important thing to remember about an _____ is that it represents a period of time.

Chapter 23. Performance Evaluation for Decentralized Operations

a. AMEX
c. Income statement
b. ABC Television Network
d. AIG

7. An _____ is a classification used for business units within an enterprise. The essential element of an _____ is that it is treated as a unit which is measured against its use of capital, as opposed to a cost or profit center, which are measured against raw costs or profits.

The advantage of this form of measurement is that it tends to be more encompassing, since it accounts for all uses of capital.

a. ABC Television Network
c. AMEX
b. AIG
d. Investment center

8. In business and accounting, _____ are everything of value that is owned by a person or company. It is a claim on the property your income of a borrower. The balance sheet of a firm records the monetary value of the _____ owned by the firm.

a. Accounts receivable
c. Accrual basis accounting
b. Earnings before interest, taxes, depreciation and amortization
d. Assets

9. _____, net margin, net _____ or net profit ratio all refer to a measure of profitability. It is calculated by finding the net profit as a percentage of the revenue.

$$\text{Net profit margin} = \frac{\text{Net profit (after taxes)}}{\text{Revenue}} \times 100$$

The _____ is mostly used for internal comparison.

a. BNSF Railway
c. 3M Company
b. BMC Software, Inc.
d. Profit margin

10. In finance, _____ also known as return on investment, rate of profit or sometimes just return, is the ratio of money gained or lost on an investment relative to the amount of money invested. The amount of money gained or lost may be referred to as interest, profit/loss, gain/loss, or net income/loss. The money invested may be referred to as the asset, capital, principal, or the cost basis of the investment.

a. Debt to capital ratio
c. Return on assets Du Pont
b. Rate of return
d. PEG ratio

11. The _____ percentage shows how profitable a company's assets are in generating revenue.

_____ can be computed as:

$$\text{ROA} = \frac{\text{Net Income - Interest Expense - Interest Tax savings}}{\text{Average Total Assets}}$$

Chapter 23. Performance Evaluation for Decentralized Operations

This number tells you what the company can do with what it has, i.e. how many dollars of earnings they derive from each dollar of assets they control. Its a useful number for comparing competing companies in the same industry.

    a. Capital recovery factor
    b. Statutory Liquidity Ratio
    c. Return of capital
    d. Return on Assets

12. In corporate finance, _____ or _____ is an estimate of true economic profit after making corrective adjustments to GAAP accounting, including deducting the opportunity cost of equity capital. _____ can be measured as Net Operating Profit After Taxes(or NOPAT) less the money cost of capital. _____ is similar in nature to that of calculating another financial performance measure - Residual Income , however, there are a few complexities involved with coming up with the elements for calculating _____ over RI such as the myriad adjustments that might be made to NOPAT before it is suitable for the formula below.
    a. Outsourcing
    b. International Monetary Fund
    c. Internal control
    d. Economic value added

13. _____ refers to the additional value of a commodity over the cost of commodities used to produce it from the previous stage of production. An example is the price of gasoline at the pump over the price of the oil in it. In national accounts used in macroeconomics, it refers to the contribution of the factors of production, i.e., land, labor, and capital goods, to raising the value of a product and corresponds to the incomes received by the owners of these factors.
    a. 3M Company
    b. Minimum wage
    c. Value added
    d. Supply-side economics

14. The _____ is a performance management tool which began as a concept for measuring whether the smaller-scale operational activities of a company are aligned with its larger-scale objectives in terms of vision and strategy.

By focusing not only on financial outcomes but also on the operational, marketing and developmental inputs to these, the _____ helps provide a more comprehensive view of a business, which in turn helps organizations act in their best long-term interests. This tool is also being used to address business response to climate change and greenhouse gas emissions.

    a. Balanced scorecard
    b. Performance measurement
    c. Cash cow
    d. Management by objectives

15. A _____ is any one of a variety of different systems, institutions, procedures, social relations and infrastructures whereby persons trade, and goods and services are exchanged, forming part of the economy. It is an arrangement that allows buyers and sellers to exchange things. _____s vary in size, range, geographic scale, location, types and variety of human communities, as well as the types of goods and services traded.
    a. Recession
    b. Nominal value
    c. Market Failure
    d. Market

16. _____ is an economic concept with commonplace familiarity. It is the price that a good or service is offered at, or will fetch, in the marketplace. It is of interest mainly in the study of microeconomics.

a. Spot rate
c. Financial instruments
b. Market price
d. Transfer agent

17. _____ refers to the pricing of contributions (assets, tangible and intangible, services, and funds) transferred within an organization. For example, goods from the production division may be sold to the marketing division, or goods from a parent company may be sold to a foreign subsidiary. Since the prices are set within an organization (i.e. controlled), the typical market mechanisms that establish prices for such transactions between third parties may not apply.
   a. Transfer pricing
   c. Target costing
   b. Resale price maintenance
   d. Transactional Net Margin Method

18. _____ in economics and business is the result of an exchange and from that trade we assign a numerical monetary value to a good, service or asset. If Alice trades Bob 4 apples for an orange, the _____ of an orange is 4 apples. Inversely, the _____ of an apple is 1/4 oranges.
   a. Resale price maintenance
   c. Pricing
   b. Price
   d. Transactional Net Margin Method

19. _____ is one of the four Ps of the marketing mix. The other three aspects are product, promotion, and place. It is also a key variable in microeconomic price allocation theory.
   a. Pricing
   c. Cost-plus pricing
   b. Target costing
   d. Price discrimination

Chapter 24. Differential Analysis and Product Pricing

1. In economics, business, retail, and accounting, a _____ is the value of money that has been used up to produce something, and hence is not available for use anymore. In economics, a _____ is an alternative that is given up as a result of a decision. In business, the _____ may be one of acquisition, in which case the amount of money expended to acquire it is counted as _____.
   a. Cost
   c. Prime cost
   b. Cost allocation
   d. Cost of quality

2. In economics and business decision-making, _____ are costs that cannot be recovered once they have been incurred. _____ are sometimes contrasted with variable costs, which are the costs that will change due to the proposed course of action, and prospective costs which are costs that will be incurred if an action is taken.

   In traditional microeconomic theory, only variable costs are relevant to a decision.

   a. 3M Company
   c. BMC Software, Inc.
   b. BNSF Railway
   d. Sunk costs

3. _____ is one of a series of accounting transactions dealing with the billing of customers who owe money to a person, company or organization for goods and services that have been provided to the customer. In most business entities this is typically done by generating an invoice and mailing or electronically delivering it to the customer, who in turn must pay it within an established timeframe called credit or payment terms.

   An example of a common payment term is Net 30, meaning payment is due in the amount of the invoice 30 days from the date of invoice.

   a. Accrual
   c. Accrued revenue
   b. Adjusting entries
   d. Accounts receivable

4. A _____ is a contract conferring a right on one person to possess property belonging to another person (called a landlord or lessor) to the exclusion of the owner landlord. It is a rental agreement between landlord and tenant. The relationship between the tenant and the landlord is called a tenancy, and the right to possession by the tenant is sometimes called a leasehold interest.
   a. Board of directors
   c. Fraud Enforcement and Recovery Act
   b. Types of business
   d. Lease

5. _____ is the total cost involved in operating all production facilities of a manufacturing business. It generally applies to indirect labor and indirect cost, it also includes all costs involved in manufacturing with the exception of the cost of raw materials and direct labor. _____ also includes certain costs such as quality assurance costs, cleanup costs, and property insurance premiums.
   a. Cost driver
   c. Profit center
   b. Contribution margin analysis
   d. Factory overhead

6. In business, _____, Overhead cost or _____ expense refers to an ongoing expense of operating a business. The term _____ is usually used to group expenses that are necessary to the continued functioning of the business, but do not directly generate profits.

   _____ expenses are all costs on the income statement except for direct labor and direct materials.

Chapter 24. Differential Analysis and Product Pricing

    a. Intangible assets
    c. Overhead
    b. ABC Television Network
    d. AIG

7. The _____ of 2002 (Pub.L. 107-204, 116 Stat. 745, enacted July 30, 2002), also known as the Public Company Accounting Reform and Investor Protection Act of 2002, is a United States federal law enacted on July 30, 2002 in response to a number of major corporate and accounting scandals including those affecting Enron, Tyco International, Adelphia, Peregrine Systems and WorldCom. The legislation establishes new or enhanced standards for all U.S. public company boards, management, and public accounting firms. It does not apply to privately held companies.
    a. Tax lien
    c. Burden of proof
    b. Staple right
    d. Sarbanes-Oxley Act

8. _____ or economic opportunity loss is the value of the next best alternative foregone as the result of making a decision. _____ analysis is an important part of a company's decision-making processes but is not treated as an actual cost in any financial statement. The next best thing that a person can engage in is referred to as the _____ of doing the best thing and ignoring the next best thing to be done.
    a. ABC Television Network
    c. Inflation
    b. AIG
    d. Opportunity cost

9. _____ in economics and business is the result of an exchange and from that trade we assign a numerical monetary value to a good, service or asset. If Alice trades Bob 4 apples for an orange, the _____ of an orange is 4 apples. Inversely, the _____ of an apple is 1/4 oranges.
    a. Resale price maintenance
    c. Price
    b. Transactional Net Margin Method
    d. Pricing

10. _____ is the difference between the cost of a good or service and its selling price. A _____ is added on to the total cost incurred by the producer of a good or service in order to create a profit. The total cost reflects the total amount of both fixed and variable expenses to produce and distribute a product.
    a. Capital
    c. Swap
    b. Fiscal
    d. Markup

11. The _____ of 1936 (or Anti-Price Discrimination Act, 15 U.S.C. § 13) is a United States federal law that prohibits what were considered, at the time of passage, to be anticompetitive practices by producers, specifically price discrimination. It grew out of practices in which chain stores were allowed to purchase goods at lower prices than other retailers.
    a. Joint venture
    c. Computer Fraud and Abuse Act
    b. Tax patent
    d. Robinson-Patman Act

12. In economics, and cost accounting, _____ describes the total economic cost of production and is made up of variable costs, which vary according to the quantity of a good produced and include inputs such as labor and raw materials, plus fixed costs, which are independent of the quantity of a good produced and include inputs (capital) that cannot be varied in the short term, such as buildings and machinery. _____ in economics includes the total opportunity cost of each factor of production in addition to fixed and variable costs.

The rate at which _____ changes as the amount produced changes is called marginal cost.

a. 3M Company
b. BMC Software, Inc.
c. Total cost
d. BNSF Railway

13. The _____ tax is a United States payroll tax imposed by the federal government on both employees and employers to fund Social Security and Medicare --federal programs that provide benefits for retirees, the disabled, and children of deceased workers. Social Security benefits include old-age, survivors, and disability insurance (OASDI); Medicare provides hospital insurance benefits. The amount that one pays in payroll taxes throughout one's working career is indirectly tied to the social security benefits annuity that one receives as a retiree.
    a. Deficit
    b. Federal tax revenue by state
    c. Tax evasion
    d. Federal Insurance Contributions Act

14. _____, in law and economics, is a form of risk management primarily used to hedge against the risk of a contingent loss. _____ is defined as the equitable transfer of the risk of a loss, from one entity to another, in exchange for a premium, and can be thought of as a guaranteed small loss to prevent a large, possibly devastating loss. An insurer is a company selling the _____; an insured is the person or entity buying the _____.
    a. AIG
    b. ABC Television Network
    c. AMEX
    d. Insurance

15. _____ is an agreement between business competitors to sell the same product or service at the same price. In general, it is an agreement intended to ultimately push the price of a product as high as possible, leading to profits for all the sellers. Price-fixing can also involve any agreement to fix, peg, discount or stabilize prices.
    a. BMC Software, Inc.
    b. 3M Company
    c. BNSF Railway
    d. Price fixing

16. _____s are expenses that change in proportion to the activity of a business. In other words, _____ is the sum of marginal costs. It can also be considered normal costs.
    a. Quality costs
    b. Fixed costs
    c. Cost accounting
    d. Variable cost

17. _____ is a costing model that identifies activities in an organization and assigns the cost of each activity resource to all products and services according to the actual consumption by each: it assigns more indirect costs (overhead) into direct costs.

In this way an organization can establish the true cost of its individual products and services for the purposes of identifying and eliminating those which are unprofitable and lowering the prices of those which are overpriced.

In a business organization, the ABC methodology assigns an organization's resource costs through activities to the products and services provided to its customers.

   a. Indirect costs
   b. ABC Television Network
   c. Activity-based management
   d. Activity-based costing

18. _____ is a pricing method used by firms. It is defined as 'a cost management tool for reducing the overall cost of a product over its entire life-cycle with the help of production, engineering, research and design'. A target cost is the maximum amount of cost that can be incurred on a product and with it the firm can still earn the required profit margin from that product at a particular selling price.

Chapter 24. Differential Analysis and Product Pricing   149

a. Target costing
b. Penetration pricing
c. Price
d. Price discrimination

19. _____ is an overall management philosophy introduced by Dr. Eliyahu M. Goldratt in his 1984 book titled The Goal, that is geared to help organizations continually achieve their goal. The title comes from the contention that any manageable system is limited in achieving more of its goal by a very small number of constraints, and that there is always at least one constraint. The _____ process seeks to identify the constraint and restructure the rest of the organization around it, through the use of the Five Focusing Steps.

a. Make to order
b. Six Sigma
c. Lean production
d. Theory of constraints

20. _____ is one of the four Ps of the marketing mix. The other three aspects are product, promotion, and place. It is also a key variable in microeconomic price allocation theory.

a. Price discrimination
b. Target costing
c. Cost-plus pricing
d. Pricing

21. In cost-volume-profit analysis, a form of management accounting, _____ is the marginal profit per unit sale. It is a useful quantity in carrying out various calculations, and can be used as a measure of operating leverage.

The Total _____ is Total Revenue (TR, or Sales) minus Total Variable Cost (TVC):

Tcontribution margin = TR − TVC

The Unit _____ (C) is Unit Revenue (Price, P) minus Unit Variable Cost (V):

C = P − V

The _____ Ratio is the percentage of Contribution over Total Revenue, which can be calculated from the unit contribution over unit price or total contribution over Total Revenue:

$$\frac{C}{P} = \frac{P-V}{P} = \frac{\text{Unit Contribution Margin}}{\text{Price}} = \frac{\text{Total Contribution Margin}}{\text{Total Revenue}}$$

For instance, if the price is $10 and the unit variable cost is $2, then the unit _____ is $8, and the _____ ratio is $8/$10 = 80%.

a. Factory overhead
b. Profit center
c. Cost driver
d. Contribution margin

Chapter 25. Capital Investment Analysis

1. In economics, _____ or _____ goods or real _____ refers to factors of production used to create goods or services that are not themselves significantly consumed (though they may depreciate) in the production process. _____ goods may be acquired with money or financial _____. In finance and accounting, _____ generally refers to financial wealth, especially that used to start or maintain a business.

   a. Debt-to-GDP ratios
   c. Sale
   b. Consumption
   d. Capital

2. _____ is the planning process used to determine whether a firm's long term investments such as new machinery, replacement machinery, new plants, new products, and research development projects are worth pursuing. It is budget for major capital, or investment, expenditures.

   Many formal methods are used in _____, including the techniques such as

   - Net present value
   - Profitability index
   - Internal rate of return
   - Modified Internal Rate of Return
   - Equivalent annuity

   These methods use the incremental cash flows from each potential investment, or project. Techniques based on accounting earnings and accounting rules are sometimes used - though economists consider this to be improper - such as the accounting rate of return, and 'return on investment.' Simplified and hybrid methods are used as well, such as payback period and discounted payback period.

   a. Capital budgeting
   c. Flow-through entity
   b. Gross profit
   d. Restricted stock

3. The arithmetic _____ over n periods is defined as:

$$\bar{r}_{arithmetic} = \frac{1}{n} \sum_{i=1}^{n} r_{arith,i} = \frac{1}{n}(r_{arith,1} + \cdots + r_{arith,n})$$

The geometric _____, also known as the time-weighted rate of return, over n periods is defined as:

$$\bar{r}_{geometric} = -1 + \prod_{i=1}^{n}(1 + r_{arith,i})^{1/n}$$

The geometric _____ calculated over n years is also known as the annualized return.

The internal rate of return, also known as the dollar-weighted rate of return, is defined as the value(s) of $\bar{r}$ that satisfies the following equation:

$$\text{NPV} = \sum_{t=0}^{n} \frac{C_t}{(1+\bar{r})^t} = 0$$

where:

- NPV = net present value of the investment
- C_t = cashflow at time t

For both arithmetic returns and logarithmic returns, an investment is profitable when either r_{arith} or r_{log} > 0, and unprofitable when either r_{arith} or r_{log} < 0.

The value of an investment is doubled over a year if the annual ROR $r_{arith} = +100\%$ or $r_{log} = \ln(2) = 69.3\%$. The value falls to zero when $r_{arith} = -100\%$ or $r_{log} = -\infty$.

a. Average rate of return
b. Earnings yield
c. Asset turnover
d. Average propensity to consume

4. _____ is the value on a given date of a future payment or series of future payments, discounted to reflect the time value of money and other factors such as investment risk. _____ calculations are widely used in business and economics to provide a means to compare cash flows at different times on a meaningful 'like to like' basis.

The most commonly applied model of the time value of money is compound interest.

a. Future value
b. Net present value
c. Present value
d. 3M Company

5. Simply put, _____ is the value of money figuring in a given amount of interest for a given amount of time. For example 100 dollars of todays money held for a year at 5 percent interest is worth 105 dollars, therefore 100 dollars paid now or 105 dollars paid exactly one year from now is the same amount of payment of money with that given intersest at that given amount of time. This notion dates at least to Martín de Azpilcueta of the School of Salamanca.

a. Collusion
b. Merck ' Co., Inc.
c. Competition law
d. Time value of money

6. In finance, _____ also known as return on investment, rate of profit or sometimes just return, is the ratio of money gained or lost on an investment relative to the amount of money invested. The amount of money gained or lost may be referred to as interest, profit/loss, gain/loss, or net income/loss. The money invested may be referred to as the asset, capital, principal, or the cost basis of the investment.

a. Return on assets Du Pont
b. Debt to capital ratio
c. PEG ratio
d. Rate of return

7. A _____ is a contract conferring a right on one person to possess property belonging to another person (called a landlord or lessor) to the exclusion of the owner landlord. It is a rental agreement between landlord and tenant. The relationship between the tenant and the landlord is called a tenancy, and the right to possession by the tenant is sometimes called a leasehold interest.

a. Fraud Enforcement and Recovery Act
b. Board of directors
c. Types of business
d. Lease

Chapter 25. Capital Investment Analysis

8. _____ is the remaining amount after deductions from the gross salary, where net means ultimate.

Example deductions: income taxes, trade union dues, authorized deduction for a retirement fund.

_____ is the amount left over after deductions from the gross salary.

a. 3M Company
c. Net pay
b. Residual value
d. Round-tripping

9. Employment is a contract between two parties, one being the employer and the other being the _____. An _____ may be defined as: 'A person in the service of another under any contract of hire, express or implied, oral or written, where the employer has the power or right to control and direct the _____ in the material details of how the work is to be performed.' Black's Law Dictionary page 471 (5th ed. 1979.)

a. AIG
c. ABC Television Network
b. AMEX
d. Employee

10. _____ in business and economics refers to the period of time required for the return on an investment to 'repay' the sum of the original investment. For example, a $1000 investment which returned $500 per year would have a two year _____. It intuitively measures how long something takes to 'pay for itself.' Shorter _____s are obviously preferable to longer _____s (all else being equal.)

a. Treasury company
c. Payback period
b. Segregated portfolio company
d. Fair market value

11. In monetary economics _____ can refer either to a particular _____, for example British Pounds or United States Dollars, or, to the coins and banknotes of a particular _____, which actually form only a small part of the monetary base of a nation's money supply. The other part of a nation's money supply consists of money deposited in banks (sometimes called deposit money), ownership of which can be transferred by means of checks (cheques in the United Kingdom and Australia) or other forms of money transfer such as credit and debit cards. Deposit money and _____ are 'money' in the sense that both are acceptable as a means of exchange, but money need not necessarily be '_____'.

a. Currency
c. BNSF Railway
b. 3M Company
d. BMC Software, Inc.

12. In economics, _____ is a rise in the general level of prices of goods and services in an economy over a period of time. When the general price level rises, each unit of currency buys fewer goods and services; consequently, _____ is also a decline in the real value of money--a loss of purchasing power in the medium of exchange which is also the monetary unit of account in the economy. A chief measure of general price-level _____ is the general _____ rate, which is the percentage change in a general price index (normally the Consumer Price Index) over time.

a. AIG
c. Opportunity cost
b. ABC Television Network
d. Inflation

13. An _____ is a term used in behavioral economics to describe those types of behaviors that impose costs on a person in the long-run that are not taken into account when making decisions in the present. Classical Economics discourages government from creating legislation that targets internalities, because it is assumed that the consumer takes these personal costs into account when paying for the good that causes the _____. For example, cigarettes should be taxed because of the negative consumption externalities that they impose, such as second-hand smoke, not because the smoker harms him or herself by smoking.

Chapter 25. Capital Investment Analysis

a. Internality
c. Authorised capital
b. Inventory turnover ratio
d. Operating budget

14. The _____ is the main body of domestic statutory tax law of the United States organized topically, including laws covering the income tax, payroll taxes, gift taxes, estate taxes and statutory excise taxes. The _____ is published as Title 26 of the United States Code (USC), and is also known as the internal revenue title.
   a. Equity of condition
   c. Internal Revenue Code
   b. Ordinary income
   d. Income tax

15. _____ is the balance of the amounts of cash being received and paid by a business during a defined period of time, sometimes tied to a specific project. Measurement of _____ can be used

   - to evaluate the state or performance of a business or project.
   - to determine problems with liquidity. Being profitable does not necessarily mean being liquid. A company can fail because of a shortage of cash, even while profitable.
   - to project rate of returns. The time of _____s into and out of projects are used as inputs to financial models such as internal rate of return, and net present value.
   - to examine income or growth of a business when it is believed that accrual accounting concepts do not represent economic realities. Alternately, _____ can be used to 'validate' the net income generated by accrual accounting.

_____ as a generic term may be used differently depending on context, and certain _____ definitions may be adapted by analysts and users for their own uses. Common terms include operating _____ and free _____.

   a. Gross income
   c. Gross profit
   b. Flow-through entity
   d. Cash flow

16. _____ in economics and business is the result of an exchange and from that trade we assign a numerical monetary value to a good, service or asset. If Alice trades Bob 4 apples for an orange, the _____ of an orange is 4 apples. Inversely, the _____ of an apple is 1/4 oranges.
   a. Price
   c. Transactional Net Margin Method
   b. Resale price maintenance
   d. Pricing

17. _____ is a term used in subtly different ways in a number of fields, including philosophy, physics, statistics, economics, finance, insurance, psychology, sociology, engineering, and information science. It applies to predictions of future events, to physical measurements already made, or to the unknown.

In his seminal work Risk, _____, and Profit University of Chicago economist Frank Knight (1921) established the important distinction between risk and _____:

   '_____ must be taken in a sense radically distinct from the familiar notion of risk, from which it has never been properly separated....

   a. Uncertainty
   c. AIG
   b. AMEX
   d. ABC Television Network

18. In finance, the _____ between two currencies specifies how much one currency is worth in terms of the other. It is the value of a foreign nation's currency in terms of the home nation's currency. For example an _____ of 102 Japanese yen to the United States dollar means that JPY 102 is worth the same as USD 1.
   a. ABC Television Network
   b. AIG
   c. AMEX
   d. Exchange rate

19. The term _____ is used in finance theory to refer to any terminating stream of fixed payments over a specified period of time. This usage is most commonly seen in academic discussions of finance, usually in connection with the valuation of the stream of payments, taking into account time value of money concepts such as interest rate and future value.

Examples of these are regular deposits to a savings account, monthly home mortgage payments and monthly insurance payments.

   a. Improvement
   b. Appropriation
   c. Annuity
   d. Intangible

20. In finance, the _____ approach describes a method of valuing a project, company, or asset using the concepts of the time value of money. All future cash flows are estimated and discounted to give their present values. The discount rate used is generally the appropriate WACC, that reflects the risk of the cashflows.
   a. 3M Company
   b. Present value
   c. Net present value
   d. Discounted cash flow

21. _____ or net present worth (NPW) is defined as the total present value (PV) of a time series of cash flows. It is a standard method for using the time value of money to appraise long-term projects. Used for capital budgeting, and widely throughout economics, it measures the excess or shortfall of cash flows, in present value terms, once financing charges are met.
   a. 3M Company
   b. Net present value
   c. Future value
   d. Present value

22. The _____ is a capital budgeting metric used by firms to decide whether they should make investments. It is also called discounted cash flow rate of return (DCFROR) or rate of return (ROR.) It is an indicator of the efficiency or quality of an investment, as opposed to net present value (NPV), which indicates value or magnitude.
   a. AMEX
   b. Internal rate of return
   c. ABC Television Network
   d. AIG

23. In mathematics _____s are numbers or other things that get multiplied. In particular, see:

   - Factorization, the decomposition of an object into a product of other objects
   - Integer factorization, the process of breaking down a composite number into smaller non-trivial divisors
   - A coefficient
   - A divisor of a particular number, or of an element of a monoid
   - A von Neumann algebra with a trivial center

Chapter 25. Capital Investment Analysis

In statistics

- _____ analysis is the study of how _____s or certain variables affect variables.

In technology:

- Human _____s, a profession that focuses on how people interact with products, tools, or procedures
- 'Functionality, Application domain, Conditions, Technology, Objects and Responsibility;', In object-oriented programming

In computer science and information technology:

- Authentication _____, a piece of information used to verify a person's identity for security purposes
- _____, a Unix command for numbers factorization
- _____ (programming language), an experimental Forth-like programming language

In television:

- The O'Reilly _____, an American talk show hosted by Bill O'Reilly on Fox News.
- The Krypton _____, a British game show hosted by Gordon Burns, formally on ITV. Also had an American version.

  a. Sale
  c. Markup
  b. Household and Dependent Care Credit
  d. Factor

24. An _____ is a tax levied on the financial income of people, corporations, or other legal entities. Various _____ systems exist, with varying degrees of tax incidence. Income taxation can be progressive, proportional, or regressive.

  a. Implied level of government service
  c. Income tax
  b. Individual Retirement Arrangement
  d. Ordinary income

25. _____ are a class of computational algorithms that rely on repeated random sampling to compute their results. _____ are often used when simulating physical and mathematical systems. Because of their reliance on repeated computation and random or pseudo-random numbers, _____ are most suited to calculation by a computer.

  a. Probability distribution
  c. Time series
  b. Statistics
  d. Monte Carlo methods

Chapter 26. Cost Allocation and Activity-Based Costing

1. _____ is the total cost involved in operating all production facilities of a manufacturing business. It generally applies to indirect labor and indirect cost, it also includes all costs involved in manufacturing with the exception of the cost of raw materials and direct labor. _____ also includes certain costs such as quality assurance costs, cleanup costs, and property insurance premiums.
   - a. Cost driver
   - b. Contribution margin analysis
   - c. Factory overhead
   - d. Profit center

2. In business, _____, Overhead cost or _____ expense refers to an ongoing expense of operating a business. The term _____ is usually used to group expenses that are necessary to the continued functioning of the business, but do not directly generate profits.

   _____ expenses are all costs on the income statement except for direct labor and direct materials.
   - a. Intangible assets
   - b. Overhead
   - c. ABC Television Network
   - d. AIG

3. The _____ is an American federal law which allows people who are not affiliated with the government to file actions against federal contractors claiming fraud against the government. The act of filing such actions is informally called 'whistleblowing.' Persons filing under the Act stand to receive a portion (usually about 15-25 percent) of any recovered damages.
   - a. Covenant
   - b. Vested
   - c. Lien
   - d. False Claims Act

4. In economics, business, retail, and accounting, a _____ is the value of money that has been used up to produce something, and hence is not available for use anymore. In economics, a _____ is an alternative that is given up as a result of a decision. In business, the _____ may be one of acquisition, in which case the amount of money expended to acquire it is counted as _____.
   - a. Cost
   - b. Cost allocation
   - c. Prime cost
   - d. Cost of quality

5. In finance, the _____ or quick ratio or liquid ratio measures the ability of a company to use its near cash or quick assets to immediately extinguish or retire its current liabilities. Quick assets include those current assets that presumably can be quickly converted to cash at close to their book values.

$$\text{Quick (Acid Test) Ratio} = \frac{\text{Cash} + \text{Marketable Securities} + \text{Accounts Receivables}}{\text{Current Liabilities}}$$

Generally, the acid test ratio should be 1:1 or better, however this varies widely by industry.

   - a. Inventory turnover
   - b. Earnings per share
   - c. Acid-test
   - d. Invested capital

6. _____ is a costing model that identifies activities in an organization and assigns the cost of each activity resource to all products and services according to the actual consumption by each: it assigns more indirect costs (overhead) into direct costs.

Chapter 26. Cost Allocation and Activity-Based Costing

In this way an organization can establish the true cost of its individual products and services for the purposes of identifying and eliminating those which are unprofitable and lowering the prices of those which are overpriced.

In a business organization, the ABC methodology assigns an organization's resource costs through activities to the products and services provided to its customers.

a. ABC Television Network
b. Indirect costs
c. Activity-based costing
d. Activity-based management

7. _____ in manufacturing is the process of converting a line or machine from running one product to another. _____ times can last from a few minutes to as much as several weeks in the case of automobile manufacturers retooling for new models. The terms set-up and _____ are sometimes used interchangeably however this usage is incorrect.

a. Cellular manufacturing
b. Deming Prize
c. Value engineering
d. Changeover

8. In accounting, _____ has a very specific meaning. It is an outflow of cash or other valuable assets from a person or company to another person or company. This outflow of cash is generally one side of a trade for products or services that have equal or better current or future value to the buyer than to the seller.

a. AMEX
b. AIG
c. ABC Television Network
d. Expense

9. A _____ is a type of business entity in which partners (owners) share with each other the profits or losses of the business undertaking in which all have invested. _____s are often favored over corporations for taxation purposes, as the _____ structure does not generally incur a tax on profits before it is distributed to the partners (i.e. there is no dividend tax levied.) However, depending on the _____ structure and the jurisdiction in which it operates, owners of a _____ may be exposed to greater personal liability than they would as shareholders of a corporation.

a. FCPA
b. Bond indenture
c. Trust indenture
d. Partnership

10. A _____, also client, buyer or purchaser is the buyer or user of the paid products of an individual or organization, mostly called the supplier or seller. This is typically through purchasing or renting goods or services.

a. BMC Software, Inc.
b. BNSF Railway
c. 3M Company
d. Customer

11. A _____ is any one of a variety of different systems, institutions, procedures, social relations and infrastructures whereby persons trade, and goods and services are exchanged, forming part of the economy. It is an arrangement that allows buyers and sellers to exchange things. _____s vary in size, range, geographic scale, location, types and variety of human communities, as well as the types of goods and services traded.

a. Market Failure
b. Recession
c. Nominal value
d. Market

12. A _____ of people or organizations sharing one or more characteristics that cause them to have similar product and/or service needs. A true market segment meets all of the following criteria: it is distinct from other segments (different segments have different needs), it is homogeneous within the segment (exhibits common needs); it responds similarly to a market stimulus, and it can be reached by a market intervention. The term is also used when consumers with identical product and/or service needs are divided up into groups so they can be charged different amounts.

    a. Market segment
    b. Customer relationship management
    c. Market segmentation
    d. Business-to-consumer

Chapter 27. Cost Management for Just-in-Time Environments

1. Just in Time could refer to the following:

   • _____, an inventory strategy that reduces in-process inventory
   • _____ compilation, a technique for improving the performance of bytecode-compiled programming systems

   a. Price-to-sales ratio
   b. Department of the Treasury
   c. Trailing
   d. Just-in-time

2. _____ or lean production, which is often known simply as 'Lean', is a production practice that considers the expenditure of resources for any goal other than the creation of value for the end customer to be wasteful, and thus a target for elimination. Working from the perspective of the customer who consumes a product or service, 'value' is defined as any action or process that a customer would be willing to pay for. Basically, lean is centered around creating more value with less work.
   a. Make to order
   b. Job order
   c. Six Sigma
   d. Lean manufacturing

3. A _____ is the period of time between the initiation of any process of production and the completion of that process. Thus the _____ for ordering a new car from a manufacturer may be anywhere from 2 weeks to 6 months. In industry, _____ reduction is an important part of lean manufacturing.
   a. BMC Software, Inc.
   b. Lead time
   c. BNSF Railway
   d. 3M Company

4. _____ refers to the additional value of a commodity over the cost of commodities used to produce it from the previous stage of production. An example is the price of gasoline at the pump over the price of the oil in it. In national accounts used in macroeconomics, it refers to the contribution of the factors of production, i.e., land, labor, and capital goods, to raising the value of a product and corresponds to the incomes received by the owners of these factors.
   a. Supply-side economics
   b. Minimum wage
   c. 3M Company
   d. Value added

5. In finance, the _____ or quick ratio or liquid ratio measures the ability of a company to use its near cash or quick assets to immediately extinguish or retire its current liabilities. Quick assets include those current assets that presumably can be quickly converted to cash at close to their book values.

$$\text{Quick (Acid Test) Ratio} = \frac{\text{Cash} + \text{Marketable Securities} + \text{Accounts Receivables}}{\text{Current Liabilities}}$$

Generally, the acid test ratio should be 1:1 or better, however this varies widely by industry.

   a. Acid-test
   b. Inventory turnover
   c. Earnings per share
   d. Invested capital

6. Employment is a contract between two parties, one being the employer and the other being the _____. An _____ may be defined as: 'A person in the service of another under any contract of hire, express or implied, oral or written, where the employer has the power or right to control and direct the _____ in the material details of how the work is to be performed.' Black's Law Dictionary page 471 (5th ed. 1979.)

a. Employee
b. AIG
c. ABC Television Network
d. AMEX

7. Build to order, often abbreviated as BTO and sometimes referred to as _____ , is a production approach where once a confirmed order for products is received, products are built. BTO is the oldest style of order fulfillment and is the most appropriate approach used for highly customised or low-volume products.

This approach is considered good for highly configured products, e.g. automobiles (Parry and Graves, 2008), computer servers, or for products where holding inventories is very expensive, e.g. aircraft.

a. Theory of constraints
b. Job order
c. Lean production
d. Make to order

8. _____ is the total cost involved in operating all production facilities of a manufacturing business. It generally applies to indirect labor and indirect cost, it also includes all costs involved in manufacturing with the exception of the cost of raw materials and direct labor. _____ also includes certain costs such as quality assurance costs, cleanup costs, and property insurance premiums.

a. Profit center
b. Cost driver
c. Contribution margin analysis
d. Factory overhead

9. In business, _____, Overhead cost or _____ expense refers to an ongoing expense of operating a business. The term _____ is usually used to group expenses that are necessary to the continued functioning of the business, but do not directly generate profits.

_____ expenses are all costs on the income statement except for direct labor and direct materials.

a. Overhead
b. ABC Television Network
c. Intangible assets
d. AIG

10. _____ refers to the structured transmission of data between organizations by electronic means. It is used to transfer electronic documents from one computer system to another (ie) from one trading partner to another trading partner. It is more than mere E-mail; for instance, organizations might replace bills of lading and even checks with appropriate _____ messages.

a. ABC Television Network
b. Electronic commerce
c. AIG
d. Electronic data interchange

11. _____ is a concept related to lean and just-in-time (JIT) production. The Japanese word _____ is a common everyday term meaning 'signboard' or 'billboard' and utterly lacks the specialized meaning that this loanword has acquired in English. According to Taiichi Ohno, the man credited with developing JIT, _____ is a means through which JIT is achieved.

a. Risk management
b. Kanban
c. Trademark
d. FIFO

Chapter 27. Cost Management for Just-in-Time Environments

12. Build to stock often abbreviated as BTS or _____, is a build-ahead production approach in which production plans are based on information of historical demand, along with sales forecast information. BTS is a typically what people associate with the industrial revolution mass production techniques, where in anticipation of demand vast quantities of goods are produced and stocked in warehouses.

Build to stock is considered good for high volume products where the demand is either seasonal or easily predicted, or both.

   a. Make to stock
   c. BNSF Railway
   b. BMC Software, Inc.
   d. 3M Company

13. In economics and business decision-making, _____ are costs that cannot be recovered once they have been incurred. _____ are sometimes contrasted with variable costs, which are the costs that will change due to the proposed course of action, and prospective costs which are costs that will be incurred if an action is taken.

In traditional microeconomic theory, only variable costs are relevant to a decision.

   a. 3M Company
   c. BMC Software, Inc.
   b. Sunk costs
   d. BNSF Railway

14. In finance, the term _____ describes the amount in cash that returns to the owners of a security. Normally it does not include the price variations, at the difference of the total return. _____ applies to various stated rates of return on stocks (common and preferred, and convertible), fixed income instruments (bonds, notes, bills, strips, zero coupon), and some other investment type insurance products (e.g. annuities.)

   a. Corporate Bond
   c. Yield
   b. Pension System
   d. Capital

15. '_____' is Step 7 of 'Philip Crosby's 14 Step Quality Improvement Process' . Although applicable to any type of enterprise, it has been primarily adopted within industry supply chains wherever large volumes of components are being purchased (common items such as nuts and bolts are good examples.)

_____ was a quality control program originated by the Denver Division of the Martin Marietta Corporation (now Lockheed Martin) on the Titan Missile program, which carried the first astronauts into space in the late 1960s.

   a. BNSF Railway
   c. 3M Company
   b. Zero defects
   d. BMC Software, Inc.

16. In economics, business, retail, and accounting, a _____ is the value of money that has been used up to produce something, and hence is not available for use anymore. In economics, a _____ is an alternative that is given up as a result of a decision. In business, the _____ may be one of acquisition, in which case the amount of money expended to acquire it is counted as _____.

   a. Cost
   c. Cost allocation
   b. Prime cost
   d. Cost of quality

Chapter 27. Cost Management for Just-in-Time Environments

17. _____ is a company-wide computer software system used to manage and coordinate all the resources, information, and functions of a business from shared data stores.

An _____ system has a service-oriented architecture with modular hardware and software units or 'services' that communicate on a local area network. The modular design allows a business to add or reconfigure modules (perhaps from different vendors) while preserving data integrity in one shared database that may be centralized or distributed.

   a. AIG
   c. ABC Television Network
   b. Enterprise resource planning
   d. AMEX

18. In finance, a _____ is a debt security, in which the authorized issuer owes the holders a debt and, depending on the terms of the _____, is obliged to pay interest (the coupon) and/or to repay the principal at a later date, termed maturity. It is a formal contract to repay borrowed money with interest at fixed intervals.

Thus a _____ is like a loan: the issuer is the borrower, the _____ holder is the lender, and the coupon is the interest.

   a. Revenue bonds
   c. Bond
   b. Zero-coupon bond
   d. Coupon rate

19. _____ is a product costing approach, used in a Just-In-Time (JIT) operating environment, in which costing is delayed until goods are finished. Standard costs are then flushed backward through the system to assign costs to products. The result is that detailed tracking of costs is eliminated.
   a. Cost management
   c. Contribution margin
   b. Profit center
   d. Backflush accounting

20. The concept of quality costs is a means to quantify the total _____-related efforts and deficiencies. It was first described by Armand V. Feigenbaum in a 1956 Harvard Business Review article.

Prior to its introduction, the general perception was that higher quality requires higher costs, either by buying better materials or machines or by hiring more labor.

   a. Cost accounting
   c. Marginal cost
   b. Cost of quality
   d. Quality costs

21. _____ is one of a series of accounting transactions dealing with the billing of customers who owe money to a person, company or organization for goods and services that have been provided to the customer. In most business entities this is typically done by generating an invoice and mailing or electronically delivering it to the customer, who in turn must pay it within an established timeframe called credit or payment terms.

An example of a common payment term is Net 30, meaning payment is due in the amount of the invoice 30 days from the date of invoice.

a. Accrued revenue
c. Adjusting entries
b. Accounts receivable
d. Accrual

22. An _____ is a term used in behavioral economics to describe those types of behaviors that impose costs on a person in the long-run that are not taken into account when making decisions in the present. Classical Economics discourages government from creating legislation that targets internalities, because it is assumed that the consumer takes these personal costs into account when paying for the good that causes the _____. For example, cigarettes should be taxed because of the negative consumption externalities that they impose, such as second-hand smoke, not because the smoker harms him or herself by smoking.

a. Inventory turnover ratio
c. Internality
b. Authorised capital
d. Operating budget

23. A _____ is a special type of bar chart where the values being plotted are arranged in descending order. The graph is accompanied by a line graph which shows the cumulative totals of each category, left to right. The chart was named for Vilfredo Pareto.

a. BNSF Railway
c. 3M Company
b. BMC Software, Inc.
d. Pareto chart

24. In engineering and manufacturing, _____ and quality engineering are used in developing systems to ensure products or services are designed and produced to meet or exceed customer requirements. Refer to the definition by Merriam-Webster for further information . These systems are often developed in conjunction with other business and engineering disciplines using a cross-functional approach.

a. BMC Software, Inc.
c. 3M Company
b. BNSF Railway
d. Quality control

25. The concept of _____ is a means to quantify the total cost of quality-related efforts and deficiencies. It was first described by Armand V. Feigenbaum in a 1956 Harvard Business Review article.

Prior to its introduction, the general perception was that higher quality requires higher costs, either by buying better materials or machines or by hiring more labor.

a. Variable cost
c. Marginal cost
b. Cost allocation
d. Quality costs

26. A _____ is the pinnacle activity involved in selling products or services in return for money or other compensation. It is an act of completion of a commercial activity.

A _____ is completed by the seller, the owner of the goods.

a. Serial bonds
c. Controlled Foreign Corporations
b. Procter ' Gamble
d. Sale

Chapter 1
1. d	2. d	3. c	4. c	5. d	6. d	7. a	8. a	9. d	10. d
11. d	12. d	13. d	14. d	15. d	16. b	17. d	18. d	19. b	20. a
21. d	22. d	23. d	24. d	25. a	26. a	27. d	28. c	29. c	30. c
31. c	32. d	33. c	34. a	35. c	36. d	37. d	38. d	39. d	40. a
41. b	42. b	43. c	44. a	45. d	46. a	47. a	48. d	49. c	50. a
51. d	52. b	53. d	54. c	55. d	56. d	57. b	58. a	59. d	60. d
61. d									

Chapter 2
1. d	2. d	3. d	4. d	5. a	6. d	7. b	8. b	9. d	10. d
11. d	12. d	13. d	14. d	15. c	16. d	17. d	18. d	19. c	20. b
21. d	22. c	23. d	24. b	25. d	26. d				

Chapter 3
1. a	2. d	3. b	4. a	5. a	6. a	7. d	8. d	9. d	10. b
11. a	12. d	13. a	14. d	15. d	16. d	17. a	18. d	19. d	20. c
21. c	22. d	23. c	24. d	25. d	26. a	27. d			

Chapter 4
1. b	2. d	3. c	4. d	5. d	6. d	7. d	8. d	9. d	10. d
11. d	12. d	13. c	14. d	15. a	16. d	17. d	18. d	19. d	20. c
21. d	22. d	23. b	24. b	25. d	26. d	27. a	28. a	29. b	30. d
31. c	32. b	33. d	34. d	35. c					

Chapter 5
1. d	2. c	3. d	4. a	5. d	6. c	7. c	8. d	9. d	10. d
11. d	12. c	13. d	14. d	15. d	16. d	17. b	18. a	19. d	20. c
21. a	22. b	23. d	24. a	25. d	26. a	27. b	28. d	29. c	30. c
31. b	32. a	33. a	34. c	35. d	36. d				

Chapter 6
1. b	2. b	3. c	4. c	5. d	6. d	7. d	8. b	9. d	10. b
11. b	12. d	13. d	14. d	15. a	16. d	17. d	18. a	19. a	20. d
21. d	22. a	23. d	24. a	25. d	26. a	27. d			

Chapter 7
1. c	2. d	3. d	4. a	5. d	6. a	7. d	8. d	9. d	10. d
11. d	12. c	13. c	14. a	15. a	16. d	17. d	18. d	19. c	20. c
21. d	22. d	23. c	24. d	25. b	26. a	27. d	28. d		

Chapter 8
1. a	2. a	3. d	4. d	5. d	6. d	7. a	8. d	9. a	10. c
11. d	12. a	13. d	14. a	15. b	16. c	17. c	18. d	19. d	20. d
21. b									

ANSWER KEY

Chapter 9
1. a	2. c	3. d	4. d	5. d	6. c	7. d	8. b	9. c	10. b
11. a	12. b	13. a	14. d	15. a	16. a	17. d	18. b	19. b	20. d
21. d	22. d	23. a	24. c	25. a	26. d	27. d	28. d	29. a	30. d
31. d	32. b	33. b	34. d	35. d	36. d	37. d	38. d	39. d	40. c

Chapter 10
1. d	2. a	3. c	4. d	5. d	6. d	7. d	8. b	9. a	10. d
11. a	12. a	13. b	14. d	15. b	16. a	17. d	18. d	19. d	20. d
21. d	22. d	23. c	24. d	25. c	26. c	27. c	28. a	29. d	30. d
31. b	32. a	33. b	34. d	35. d	36. b	37. c	38. d	39. d	40. b
41. d	42. b	43. d	44. d	45. d	46. d				

Chapter 11
1. d	2. d	3. d	4. d	5. c	6. c	7. d	8. d	9. d	10. c
11. a	12. d	13. d	14. c	15. d	16. d	17. d	18. d	19. d	20. a
21. d	22. b	23. c	24. c	25. d	26. b	27. d	28. c	29. d	30. b
31. c	32. a	33. c	34. b	35. b	36. c	37. d	38. d	39. d	40. c

Chapter 12
1. a	2. d	3. d	4. d	5. d	6. c	7. b	8. c	9. d	10. c
11. d	12. a	13. a	14. c	15. d	16. c	17. d	18. d	19. a	20. c
21. b	22. d	23. b	24. c	25. d	26. d	27. c	28. c	29. d	30. b
31. d	32. c	33. b	34. c	35. d	36. b	37. d	38. b	39. d	

Chapter 13
1. a	2. b	3. d	4. d	5. b	6. d	7. d	8. c	9. d	10. d
11. d	12. d	13. a	14. d	15. d	16. a	17. d	18. d	19. b	20. c
21. d	22. d	23. b	24. d	25. a	26. d	27. d	28. d	29. d	30. a
31. d	32. d	33. d	34. d						

Chapter 14
1. c	2. c	3. c	4. d	5. d	6. c	7. d	8. a	9. a	10. a
11. d	12. a	13. d	14. d	15. d	16. d	17. a	18. d	19. d	20. a
21. d	22. d	23. a	24. a	25. d	26. a	27. b			

Chapter 15
1. c	2. d	3. d	4. b	5. c	6. d	7. c	8. a	9. d	10. d
11. d	12. c	13. b	14. a	15. b	16. c	17. c	18. d	19. b	20. a
21. d	22. c	23. a	24. d	25. d	26. d	27. d	28. d	29. d	30. d
31. b	32. b	33. a	34. c	35. b	36. d	37. a	38. d		

Chapter 16
1. a   2. b   3. c   4. d   5. b   6. c   7. b   8. d   9. b   10. c
11. a   12. d   13. d   14. d   15. b   16. d   17. b   18. c   19. d   20. c
21. a   22. a   23. c   24. d   25. b   26. d   27. b   28. d

Chapter 17
1. d   2. d   3. d   4. c   5. d   6. a   7. a   8. d   9. d   10. b
11. b   12. d   13. d   14. a   15. b   16. d   17. b   18. d   19. d   20. a

Chapter 18
1. c   2. c   3. a   4. a   5. d   6. a   7. d   8. a   9. d

Chapter 19
1. d   2. d   3. c   4. d   5. d   6. c   7. d   8. b   9. d   10. a
11. d   12. d   13. a   14. d

Chapter 20
1. d   2. a   3. b   4. c   5. d   6. c   7. b   8. d   9. a   10. d
11. a   12. d   13. a   14. a   15. d

Chapter 21
1. a   2. b   3. b   4. b   5. d   6. d   7. b   8. b   9. c   10. d
11. b   12. b   13. d   14. a   15. b   16. d   17. d   18. d

Chapter 22
1. d   2. a   3. a   4. d   5. d   6. d   7. d   8. c   9. a   10. b
11. d   12. d

Chapter 23
1. b   2. d   3. b   4. c   5. a   6. c   7. d   8. d   9. d   10. b
11. d   12. d   13. c   14. a   15. d   16. b   17. a   18. b   19. a

Chapter 24
1. a   2. d   3. d   4. d   5. d   6. c   7. d   8. d   9. c   10. d
11. d   12. c   13. d   14. d   15. d   16. d   17. d   18. a   19. d   20. d
21. d

Chapter 25
1. d   2. a   3. a   4. c   5. d   6. d   7. d   8. c   9. d   10. c
11. a   12. d   13. a   14. c   15. d   16. a   17. a   18. d   19. c   20. d
21. b   22. b   23. d   24. c   25. d

ANSWER KEY

Chapter 26
1. c 2. b 3. d 4. a 5. c 6. c 7. d 8. d 9. d 10. d
11. d 12. c

Chapter 27
1. d 2. d 3. b 4. d 5. a 6. a 7. d 8. d 9. a 10. d
11. b 12. a 13. b 14. c 15. b 16. a 17. b 18. c 19. d 20. b
21. b 22. c 23. d 24. d 25. d 26. d

www.ingramcontent.com/pod-product-compliance
Lightning Source LLC
Chambersburg PA
CBHW082203230426
43672CB00015B/2888